TABLE OF CONTENTS

I0448885

MILITARY INTERVENTION DURING THE CLINTON ADMINISTRATION
A CRITICAL COMPARISON

Military interventions are not a new phenomenon. From 1798 until 1993 when President William Clinton took office, on at least 228 occasions the "United States used its armed forces abroad in conflict, potential conflict, or for other than normal peace time purposes."[1] Justifications for such interventions and the behavior of the United States (U.S.) toward other countries are "rooted in the pursuit, protection and promotion of its interests."[2] Charged with protecting these interests, U.S. presidents often find themselves struggling to identify those interests, sometimes describing them to suit ideological bents or sometimes exhibiting warped perceptions of those interests. In order to understand and perhaps act upon the President's view of "worldwide interests, goals and objectives of the United States that are vital to the national security of the United States," Congress requires from the President an annual report on National Security Strategy (NSS).[3] As part of the report, Congress also requires the President to describe U.S. foreign policy and worldwide commitments necessary to support the national security strategy. Since the National Security Strategy Report (NSSR) was first required in 1986, most presidents have used it to describe their rationale for the employment of military force and as a policy basis to take action.

During his eight-year administration, President Clinton repeatedly faced situations where forces and events challenged U.S. interests and values. In some cases, the use of force was the selected option; then in other cases, the administration rejected the use of force. The Rwandan genocide crisis of 1994 and the ethnic cleansing crisis that occurred in Kosovo during 1998 and 1999 provide two unique, yet similar cases, for examining the Clinton administration's use of military intervention. Examining the cases may answer the fundamental question of what drove military intervention during President Clinton's administration.

This Strategic Research Paper (SRP) will measure the Clinton administration's approach to military intervention by comparing and contrasting the Rwandan genocide crisis of 1994 and the Kosovo crisis of 1999. Before looking at the cases, it discusses U.S. national interests and the Clinton administration's NSS. Later it introduces criteria for interventions – which include five interrelated areas: ideology, the global system, public and elite convictions, mass media, and finally policy inertia – as a basis for comparing the two crises.[4] Before assessing the cases, the paper provides a background for each crisis in an effort to understand their sources and apply the criteria. Conclusions seek to answer to the question of why the U.S. intervened militarily to stop ethnic cleansing in Kosovo but did not intervene to stop genocide in Rwanda.

This SRP is limited to two specific cases and brief background of national security issues. It does not directly address other National Military Strategy topics. The background discussions of the case studies are necessarily brief. Detailed discussions of both crises can be found in several extensive studies, especially Alan J. Kuperman's, balanced account of the Rwandan genocide, The Limits of Humanitarian Intervention; and Gerard Prunier's detailed account, The Rwanda Crisis. Regarding Kosovo, William T. Johnsen's short book Deciphering the Balkan Enigma: Using History to Inform Policy provides an excellent insight into the historical nature of Balkan conflict while General Wesley Clark's, Waging Modern War, provides an informed view of national interests leading to U.S. intervention.

U.S. NATIONAL INTERESTS AND NATIONAL SECURITY STRATEGY

U.S. NATIONAL INTERESTS

U.S. national interests form the basis of our foreign relations. They are derived from the way we see ourselves as a people, from our concept of national values, and from our Constitution. Interpretation of the interests leads to the ways and means by which pursue policy objectives. "Under the U.S. Constitutional system the President has the primary responsibility to define national interests with the advice and consent of the Senate and with the financial support from the Senate and House."[5] How a President defines those interests depends largely on his political leanings.

Most thoughts on U.S. interests reflect variations of realist and idealist theories. Contemporary U.S. realist views are generally associated with the scholar Hans Morgenthau who claimed, "International politics, like all politics, is a struggle for power."[6] Conversely, contemporary idealists usually trace their lineage back to President Woodrow Wilson who "despised as amoral or even immoral approaches that used power, national interest and recourse to violence as normal components of international relations."[7] Wilsonian idealism focused on making the "world free for democracy," by observance of the tenets of international law to ensure the self-determination of oppressed peoples. Because of their fundamental differences, each school sponsored different approaches to foreign policy. For example, Wilsonian thought was based on "ethical and normative approaches" and "steeped in what George F. Kennan called a 'legal-moralistic approach.'"[8] While Morgentau approached foreign policy solely in terms of national interest of which he "saw only two levels, vital and secondary" and then "distinguished them as temporary and permanent.[9] Still other realists like Donald Neuchterlein categorized basic national interests as defense of the homeland, economic well

2

being, favorable world order, and promotion of values. He applied levels of intensity (survival, vital, major and peripheral) to perceived threats to basic enduring interests as a means to determine U.S. stakes.[10] While the categories require little definition, determining degrees of intensity has seen much debate. As we shall see, it was in the Clinton administration's inability to initially determine and then apply the levels of intensity that invited criticism of its foreign policy.

NATIONAL SECURITY STRATEGY.

In 1986, as part of the Goldwater-Nichols Defense Reorganization Act, Congress added the requirement for the president to provide a written vision of his National Security Strategy. The annual document typically addresses the ends, ways, and means by which the president intends to accomplish his administration's strategy. Don M. Snider, a former National Security Council staff member responsible for preparation of the 1988 NSSR, states that the report serves five primary purposes: communicate the President's strategic vision to Congress; communicate the same vision to foreign constituencies, many of which are not on U.S. summit agendas; communicate to selected domestic audiences interested in seeing their interests articulated; communicate to the internal Executive Branch constituency a consensus of foreign and defense policies in order to support the President's agenda; and, lastly, contribute to the overall Presidential agenda.[11] Snider also identifies downsides to the document: Skeptics claim that the static, annual report is of limited value to an administration trying to articulate a vision, given the speed of world events and a sometimes hostile Congress and media.[12] Despite its shortcomings, the report nonetheless provides a single source of an administration's NSS policies.

President Clinton published his first NSS in July 1994, almost a year and half into his first administration. There were several reasons why it took so long for the administration to publish its first report. Among them was a lack of consensus within the administration, a lack of guidance and attention to foreign policy by the President, an inefficient national security apparatus within the Executive Branch, and Congressional politics resulting from a close presidential election.[13]

Before it published its first Report, the Clinton administration articulated national interests through speeches, hearings, and Presidential Decision Directives (PDD). For example, in his January 1993 confirmation hearing, Secretary of State Warren Christopher identified three principles as the pillars of the Clinton vision: economic security, a strong military, and support for global democracy.[14] Those pillars formed the basis for the administration's July 1994

3

NSSR's central goals. Likewise, in series of September 1993 speeches, the Clinton administration began to articulate its policy of engagement and enlargement.[15] While the publication of the 1994 NSSR followed the outbreak of genocide in Rwanda, it represents the general ideas of the administration as articulated by the President and members of his National Security Council, before and during the Rwandan genocide period. In the 1994 Report's preface, President Clinton asserted, that in pursuing his administration's goals over its first seventeen months, the strategy presented in the document "guided this effort."[16]

The July 1994 NSSR entitled "A National Security Strategy of Engagement and Enlargement" focused on what it called "new threats and new opportunities."[17] Engagement referred to the administration's focus on internationalism while enlargement described a vision of expanding the community of democratic states. The strategy's primary goals were akin to previous administration speeches: credibly sustaining American security with military forces that were ready to fight, bolstering America's economic revitalization, and promoting democracy abroad.[18] Yet there was a subtle, but important, difference between the speeches and 1994 Report. World events had already reordered the priorities of his administration's three principles. Instead of economic security having primacy over diplomacy and a strong military, "the traditional political-military emphasis gained increased primacy among the key objectives or principles."[19]

The document was a mixture of multilateralism and realism. According to the report, "the only responsible U.S. strategy [to enhance our security] is one that seeks to ensure U.S. influence over and participation in collective decision-making in a wide and growing range of circumstances."[20] To enhance security, the strategy called for the military to prepare to participate in multilateral peace enforcement efforts to broker settlements of internal conflicts. However, in the same section of the Report was a caveat: PDD 25, "U.S. Policy on Reforming Multilateral Peace Operations." According to the Report, PDD 25 was based on a "year-long interagency policy review and extensive consultations with dozens of Members of Congress from both parties."[21] Left unstated was the suspicion that the PDD resulted from criticism of the Clinton administration's, and the United Nation's (U.N.), handling of the Somali humanitarian operation seven months earlier. The PDD argued for U.S. participation in peace operations only if the operations supported U.S. interests, if their end states were tied to clear objectives and realistic criteria, and if the consequences of inaction were considered unacceptable.[22] The PDD, like the Weinberg doctrine used by the two previous Republican presidential administrations, offered specific guidelines for intervention. Before using military force, the

4

Weinberg doctrine required identification of a vital U.S. interest, public support, overwhelming force, and, significantly, a clear purpose and exit strategy. Still, a noted shortcoming of the 1994 NSSR was its globalist approach of selective engagement of U.S. interests without clearly establishing regional priorities or causes calling for military involvement.[23] Critics called it "less a strategy and more a statement of principles."[24] After the 1994 NSSR, "President Clinton offered no new broad overview of strategic security policy."[25] Instead, he usually responded to crises by delivering speeches directly addressing the issue.

By December 1998, President Clinton had published five NSSs and after the conclusion of the Kosovo air war published two NSSRs addressing U.S. security interests in the Balkans. The 1997 and 1998 versions of the NSSR, were both entitled "A National Security Strategy for a New Century," set the same goals as those enumerated in the 1994 strategy; "enhancing security, bolstering economic prosperity and promoting democracy abroad."[26] The two later documents revealed an increased emphasis on identifying American foreign policy priorities, perhaps because of criticism of "both the written and implemented foreign policies of the first Clinton administration."[27] The 1997 report called for increased "American leadership and engagement," arguing that the Balkans region was vital to U.S. security.[28] Reacting to the criticisms of inaction "in Rwanda and heartened by apparent success in Bosnia, the 1997 Report also put priority on what it called 'the Imperative of Engagement' arguing that 'American leadership and engagement in the world are vital to our security.'"[29] Echoing this argument, the 1997 Report proclaimed, "Taking reasonable risks for peace keeps us from being drawn into far more costly conflicts," then asserting that "European stability is vital to our own"[30] The 1998 Report followed up by restating that the security of Europe remains tied to "peace and stability in the Balkans."[31] Representing the inclinations of the second Clinton administration's foreign policy team, the report stated, "We must be prepared and willing to use all appropriate instruments of national power." To identify crises that called for possible use of the military instrument, the administration continued to postulate the three categories of interests (vital, important and humanitarian) first articulated in the 1995 Report. These, of course, reflect the realist views of Neuchterlein.

AGENDA SELECTION

Presidential authority does not include the privilege of arbitrarily selecting the issues that will dominate an administration's agenda. Invariably, crises shape and reshape presidential policy. The determination of a crisis and an administration's reaction to such an event reflect the degree to which an administration has already identified a policy governing the crisis and the manner in which internal and external factors influence policy. Roskin cites five interrelated criteria to structure the discussion on how national security policy is implemented, especially to warrant military intervention: ideology, the global system, public and elite convictions, mass media, and policy inertia.[32]

Ideology is defined as "a plan to improve society, or at least a claim to able to do so."[33] For purposes of this paper, ideology also accounts for the breadth of the administration's approach to foreign policy. Ideology may encourage foreign policy based on unilateralism or multilateralism and idealism or realism. Indeed, there is an ongoing ideological split within the Democratic Party between pure idealists' and pragmatists, who believe "that principle is only the starting point for effective governing."[34] Without abdicating their idealist principles, pragmatists are "acutely sensitive to the resource and time constraints" that foreign interventions have on the accomplishment of their domestic programs.[35]

The global system describes how the world operates and how countries interact with one another and with regional and international organizations. It takes into account that even a hegemonic nation like the U.S. is forced to respect the interests of its partners if it expects to keep an alliance together. Conversely, it recognizes that many alliance partners "feel little obligation to make the national interests of the hegemon their own."[36] In addition, it recognizes that a country must prioritize its interests or risk over-extending its ability to influence. For example, the United States is currently in a position analogous to late 19th century Britain's, when its "universal commerce circumscribed rather than widened Britain's field of action" because "acting on every interest would involve Britain simultaneously in some 40 wars.[37]

Convictions take in to account the "culture, values and convictions" of different segments of society and their influence on a country's reaction to events outside its borders.[38] Conviction groups include Congress, politicians, political appointees, and the public with their varied opinions and interest groups. Congress has a long-standing and important role to play in foreign policy and national security. It also has constitutional responsibilities in authorizing actions and appropriating funds. Congressional support for regions and foreign countries is often based on "cultural or ethnic affinities" of a constituency and the level of interest they have or can raise.[39] Conversely, a lack of public interest in foreign affairs can lead to a lack of focus on foreign affairs by a government. Also, the leanings of key individuals among an administration's foreign policy team along with the influence of economic elites, inside and out of the administration, can have significant impact on U.S. actions abroad. The power of key personalities is an important aspect of policy formulation. Whether a policy is in the country's best interest is not necessarily the deciding factor when strong personalities voice equally strong convictions. Additionally, large corporations can translate U.S. business interests abroad into U.S. foreign policy, as can special interest groups.[40] In part, events and a political leader's actions and inactions shape public opinion, depending on their portrayal by the mass media.

Mass media has the ability to form and shape public opinion. However, its abilities to do so fairly, accurately, and through "calm calculation" are questionable based on the competitive nature of the media and the very nature of news.[41] Likewise, there is significant unresolved debate on the whether the media, commonly referred to as "the CNN effect," actually affects policy decisions. While its ability to make policy is questionable, the vast majority of American media representatives consider themselves part of the fourth estate of government, supported by a mandate provided by the Fourth Amendment to the Constitution. They believe that they can act as a catalyst to shape policy if the circumstances are right.[42] Mass media organizations operate in a very competitive business arena and in a time-driven environment where television is the dominating force. Television can evoke strong emotions and reactions as it continuously transmits images into homes around the world. In some cases print media – broadly defined as newspapers, magazines and books – can do the same. However, with its generally increasing level of analysis, print media tends to lose out in immediacy and impact when compared to television.[43]

Lastly, policy inertia can affect an administration's foreign policy outcomes. "Once a policy is set it takes on a life of its own and may continue indefinitely" since the very nature of bureaucracy is to continue in a set direction unless there is significant redirection, strong leadership or forceful change imposed.[44] The inability of an administration to clearly communicate new policy and effectively monitor its implementation can have significant implications for policy outcomes. Likewise, within an administration, a misunderstanding of policy can lead to ineffective presidential agendas, or worse.

RWANDA

BACKGROUND

The Rwandan genocide crisis of 1994 is considerably a product of Rwanda's history. Rwanda is a historical African kingdom consisting of two distinct classes of people who originate from the same tribe: a Tutsi minority and Hutu majority. Early in its history, the two classes coexisted peacefully. But eventually the Tutsis, assisted at times by colonial powers, dominated Rwandan life. The Tutsi class headed the government, led the army, and was traditionally involved in raising cattle. On the other hand the Hutus were typically soldiers and farmers.[45] In

1899, Rwanda became part of German East Africa and remained so until it became a Belgian colony after World War I. For the most part, the Belgians ruled Rwanda lightly and supported the class system by leaving the minority Tutsi in charge.[46] Significantly, during this early period the Belgians began requiring all Rwandans to carry identity cards labeling the owner as Tutsi or Hutu. This identification system then became a means for the Hutus to easily identify and kill Tutsis before and during the genocide.[47] Also during their colonial period, the Belgians, along with the Catholic Church, established an educational system that included both Tutsis and Hutus. Over time, this system educated a Hutu group that would later work to eradicate their historical Tutsi rulers.[48]

As Belgium began to give up their colonial hold in the late 1950s, a political system based on ethnicity began to emerge. Believing that the Tutsis were leaning toward communism, the Belgians shifted their support to the Hutu majority and its political party.[49] This shift in support increased the tension between the two peoples and opposing parties. In 1962, conflict erupted as the Hutus sought and gained independence from both the Belgians and the ruling Tutsi class. The formation of political parties along ethnic lines is considered a fundamental reason for the ethnic massacres that have occurred in Rwanda since 1962. "Until political parties formed on the basis of ethnic origins there were no massacres of either group by the other" but by 1964, almost 70 percent of the Rwandan Tutsi population had fled to neighboring countries; and by 1967, 20,000 Tutsis had already died in ethnic conflict.[50]

These early refugees became the founders of the Rwandan Patriotic Front (RPF), the exiled Tutsis that brought return of Tutsi rule to Rwanda following the genocide. For almost 31 years, the Tutsi exiles battled the Hutu leadership of Rwandan government, first the Kayibanda government and then, following a 1973 coup d'etat, the Habyarimana government. During this time, the RPF also added to regional instability by using neighboring Uganda and Burundi as operating bases. Compounding the problem, both Uganda and Burundi were experiencing their own ethnic conflict between Hutu and Tutsi. During its eleven-year reign, the Kayibanda government often employed ethnic hatred as a means to ensure power. After the Habyarimana government seized power in 1973, Rwanda enjoyed a period of relative stability and lessened ethnic tension. However, with the worldwide collapse of coffee prices in the late 1980s, tensions increased as Habyarimana used the ethnic card to deflect blame for the ensuing poor economic conditions within Rwanda.[51]

In 1990, the RPF attacked into Rwanda to seize power, but the Habyarimana government, with the support of Zairian and French troops, repelled them. The attack, however, along with later RPF successes, triggered concerted efforts by the Organization for African Unity (OAU), the U.N. and neighboring countries to seek a peace. For its part, in June 1993 the U.N. adopted U.N. Resolution (UNR) 846 creating the United Nations Observer Mission Uganda/Rwanda (UNOMUR) with a mandate to stem the arms flow from Uganda into Rwanda. In August 1993, the OAU oversaw a negotiated end to the civil war with the Arusha Peace Accords.[52] The U.N. supported the Arusha Accords by passing UNR 872, which created the U.N. Assistance Mission for Rwanda (UNAMIR). The Belgian, Ghanaian, and Bangladeshi troops who were initially part of UNOMUR then became the basis for UNAMIR. Likewise, a separate OAU Neutral Military Observer Group was integrated into UNAMIR, giving it a troop strength of about 2,500.[53] Under the command of Canadian Lieutenant General Dallaire, UNAMIR's mission was to oversee the peace between the two formerly warring parties. As part of the accords, President Habyarimana would remain president and would share power with the members of the RPF opposition under U.N. supervision. However, U.N. presence did not prevent continuing violence between the parties and in the region. In October 1993, Tutsi rebels in neighboring Burundi staged a failed coup, killing the Hutu president and causing thousands to flee. In December 1993, Dallaire received an ominous letter warning of a plan to kill Tutsis to prevent implementation of the Arusha Accords. Then in February 1994, government troops killed a moderate Hutu cabinet minister along with 40 Tutsi.[54]

On 6 April 1994, Habyarimana and the Burundi president, returning from regional conference, died after their plane was shot down, probably by Hutus opposed to the peace accords.[55] Within an hour of the president's plane being shot down, the militia-like Interahamwe, translated as "those who work together," had established roadblocks and were searching house to house to achieve the "final solution."[56] The "final solution" was an attempt by Hutu extremist organizations, a complex mix of hate organizations including Forces Armees Rwandaises (FAR) and Interahamwe, to derail the Arusha Accords and prevent the RPF from taking over the country.[57] Using previously distributed death-lists, they began murdering both Tutsi and moderate Hutus who supported democratization. Meanwhile, RPF troops stationed in Kigali as part of the Arusha Accords began battling FAR troops in Kigali, while other RPF elements attacked south from their bases in northern Rwanda.[58]

This preplanned genocide began first in Kigali and eventually made its way out to the countryside where most Rwandans lived. Because of the unrest in Kigali, most western nations evacuated their nationals, and most humanitarian organizations sheltered themselves in their Kigali compounds to avoid the violence. Nearly all remaining media did likewise. This lack of Western presence left the global media reporting much of the killing, even reports of 20,000 dead, not as genocide but as unfortunate deaths in a continued bloody civil war centered on control of Kigali. Strangely, no refugees were seen in neighboring countries, nor were nongovernmental organizations or RPF officials making claims of genocide.[59] European newspapers that had been providing continuous coverage since April 6 "started to ignore it on April 18," believing that the civil war – related violence had stopped, when in fact it had just peaked in the countryside.[60] This lack of understanding went on for about two weeks. In the U.S., "only on April 25 did the New York Times solve the riddle, reporting that violence had 'widened into what appears to be methodical killing of Tutsi across the countryside.' The missing refugees 'either have been killed or are trying to hide.'"[61] By then most of the killing had already taken place.

The original UNAMIR mission was authorized under Chapter VI of the U.N. charter which provided it a peacekeeping mandate and did not authorize direct action to stop what was perceived as hostilities between warring parties. Dallaire and the Belgian government attempted to modify the U.N. mandate and increase UNAMIR's troop strength all through February. Despite the signs of a planned genocide, the U.S. and United Kingdom blocked Belgium's efforts, fearing results similar to the failed U.N. peace operation in Somalia where 18 American soldiers died attempting to enforce a U.N. mandate.[62] On 7 April, after Hutu extremists killed ten Belgian peacekeepers along with the Rwanda's moderate prime minister and without U.S. support in the U.N., the Belgians quickly withdrew their troops. Two weeks later, on 21 April 1994, the United Nations supported the Belgian decision by passing UNR 912 and withdrawing the majority of UNAMIR, leaving only 270 on the ground.[63]

Meanwhile, the genocide and civil war continued. FAR and militia Hutu extremist organizations drove Hutus into bordering Zaire, seeking to leave the new government with no one in Rwanda to govern. "In Butare, the militiamen ordered everyone to flee and those who refused were killed on the spot.'[64] Paradoxically, the RPF military success helped end the genocide and created an environment that eventually restored foreign intervention. In early June, the French announced their intent to conduct an operation to provide a safe haven in western Rwanda for refugees fleeing the rebels attacking from the north and east. Called Operation Turquoise, it soon received a U.N. mandate under UNR 929, along with the support of the U.S.[65] However, the operation was politically motivated, rather than a humanitarian effort. It is now known more for its success in protecting and supporting the genocidaires than helping Rwandan refugees.[66] Arriving at refugee camps in eastern Zaire, the perpetrators of the genocide claimed that they were the victims and were simply protecting themselves and their families from the RPF. Once in refugee camps, the situation worsened with a cholera outbreak. Then as Hutu extremists began to reorganize, they terrorized the other refugees, often taking

10

charge of food and medicine provided by relief organizations to leverage their control within the camps. Drawn by lines of refugees and large numbers of dead and dying, the media swarmed into Goma to cover the human catastrophe. It was not until late July, after the killing had stopped and the situation had evolved into a refugee and health concern that the United States announced that it would begin a relief operation to ease the suffering, belatedly saving some lives. By the end of a 100-day period, begun on April 6, the U.N. estimates that over 800,000 Rwandans were systematically killed.[67]

REASONS FOR U.S. INACTION INVOLVING RWANDAN GENOCIDE.

Ideology

Clinton came into office with an idealist's view of the world and a desire to pursue a multilateralist approach to foreign affairs. In 1992, candidate Clinton declared "the cynical calculus of pure power politics is ill suited to a new era."[68] By 1993, "Somalia had become the test case" for an administration that "was committed to a world-wide, assertive U.N. peacekeeping role and nation building and fostering democracy as part of U.S. national policy."[69] However, nine months into his administration and six months prior to the Rwanda genocide, the Clinton administration received a setback when 18 U.S. Army Rangers died in Somalia while enforcing a U.S.-supported U.N. mandate. Even before this catastrophe, Congress was pressuring the administration to explain its Somali policy.

Nonetheless, the administration was unprepared for the magnitude of the event and quickly withdrew its support for the mission. As Stephen Walt wrote in March 2000, the administration's ideology of "social work" was "easily swayed by . . . the public opinion polls and media buzz".[70] It seemed the administration had succumbed to ideological paralysis as it dealt with the crisis and began to rethink its foreign policy. If the incident in Somalia had not occurred, perhaps the administration's human rights concerns would have prompted substantial involvement in Rwanda.[71] The impact on an administration that was rhetorically committed "to a more aggressive use of the U.N. to rebuild failed states and to promote democratic values" cannot be overstated.[72] A multilateralist intervention gone bad, along with weakened idealist convictions, left Rwanda standing in the lurch as the administration stepped back from its ideology.

Global systems

The global system affected the U.S. response to the Rwandan crises in several areas. During the Cold War, the U.S. focused its interest in Africa on the issue of blocking Soviet expansion into the region. In the post-Cold War period, U.S. economic and military power enabled freedom of movement, much different from the Cold War period where clear priorities imposed discipline.[73] In effect, the U.S. was left with little interest in Africa, which allowed it to focus on other challenges while relying on others to administer to the region's needs.

During the 1992 election campaign, two of the major foreign policy issues were the Balkans and Haiti. They continued to be issues for much of Clinton's first administration, taking much of the time and energy he devoted to foreign policy. Africa simply was not an interest. It exhibited none of the economic factors necessary to meet the administration's vision of enlargement.[74] Nor was it included in the vision of selective engagement. As the 1994 NSSR asserted, "Africa is one of our greatest challenges for a strategy of engagement and enlargement."[75] Given the domestic focus of the president, the U.S. foreign policy focused on Haiti, close to home and closely covered by the media. Also, there was much greater probability of success in Haiti, rather than Rwanda. The administration was seeking a way to recover politically from Somalia with little threat of loss of life. Secretary of State Warren Christopher admitted some years later, that "in the early years of the Clinton administration, our concentration on Bosnia and Haiti may have drawn our attention away from the killings in Rwanda."[76]

Reliance on in-place global systems, without regard to the second-and third-order effects, may have contributed to the genocide. The administration's lack of interest in Africa, other than in its rhetoric, and the demonstrated interest of certain European countries provided the U.S. the opportunity to share the burden of Africa with its allies. Belgium and France both have long-standing complex historical ties to Africa. The willingness of Belgium to intervene early on as part of UNMOUR and UNAMIR reflects part of that history. Likewise, Frances involvements in Rwanda and Zaire, before and during the genocide, have much to do with their historical ties to these Francophones. But the problem with this arrangement is that the historical ties were also contributing to the genocide. Belgian colonialism fostered ethnic cleavage and contributed to the beginnings of the civil war. Interahamwe militiamen were in some cases trained by French military forces and the same French forces saved the Habyarimana government from defeat in 1990.[77]

The U.S. also relied on international organizations like the OAU and U.N. to address most African issues. However, the U.N.'s experience in Somalia also negatively impacted the U.N.'s outlook toward peacekeeping, resulting in only lukewarm support for intervening in Rwanda. In the 1995 edition of an Agenda for Peace, the fundamental policy document on U.N. peacekeeping, "Secretary-General Boutros Boutros Ghali expressed less optimism about possibility for intervention than he did in the 1992 (first) edition, largely because of the United Nations' searing experience in Somalia."[78] Further, the initial portrayal of the crisis as a civil war rather than genocide contributed to the lack of U.N. response. Noting the lack of U.S. support for intervention the Rwandan (Hutu) government, which was facilitating the genocide and also at the time a temporary member of the Security Council, was not going to argue for intervention.[79]

In addition, the very nature of the U.N. organization made it the least likely instrument for a quick response to the genocide. Continuous calls for a standing U.N. military force are an acknowledgement of the organizational limitations and resulting slowness of the U.N. in peacekeeping operations. This is seen in the increased reliance on regional alliances or surrogates to conduct peacekeeping and peace enforcement. Africa, however, lacked such capable organizations. A global system that offered limited alliance capability in the region, the lack of U.N. response, a lack of real interest by the major powers, the tainted nature of those that did involve themselves – all of these systemic global factors contributed to the non-responses to Rwanda's genocide.

Public and Elite convictions

Public and elite convictions affected Rwanda in a number of ways. Among them was a lack of interest in foreign policy, a wariness of civil wars, a lack of information, and an inexperienced president and foreign policy team. Public interest in foreign news stories has been dropping since the end of the Cold War. For example, the percentage of people who said they followed foreign news stories dropped from 80 percent in the 1980s to 20 percent in 1997."[80] However, this does not equate to a complete lack of interest. Polls show that there is a public interest in foreign affairs if the description of foreign affairs includes "global social and humanitarian issues that they might not always describe as foreign affairs."[81] The manner in which government and media portray foreign affairs issues influences the level of public interest. Initially, both the media and the administration presented the crisis as a civil war, not a humanitarian crisis or genocide.

The public and Congress were wary of intervening in civil wars. As we have noted, the Rwandan crisis occurred six months after the U.S. withdrew from Somalia during a U.N. mandated peace enforcement operation. The U.N. and U.S., in their "attempts to arrest [Gen. Mohammed Farah] Aidid undermined public support for humanitarian operations" involving the use of force and "paved the way for even more tragic failure in Rwanda."[82] The resulting efforts by Congress to restrict U.S. contributions to U.N. peacekeeping or deny U.S. support were a result of "perceived failures in Somalia."[83] The U.S. Congress and public, not fully aware of

13

what the administration and the U.N. were doing in Somalia, wanted a deeper explanation for any future U.S. involvement in foreign military operations. During the Rwandan genocide, there was no such explanation. Because there was also hesitancy by the administration to be involved again in an undefined peace operation, it failed to make a pubic case for any involvement and in fact resisted U.S. and U.N. participation. This did not mean that the public was completely against supporting humanitarian operations or peace operations for humanitarian purposes but they needed to be informed of the rationale and risks of any such operation.

If the public had on-going interest in humanitarian issues, why then did the American public react with such little concern for the genocide? The public was simply not fully aware of what was occurring. This occurred for at least two reasons. First, the media did not provide the means to inform. Second, the administration, which arguably did know genocide was occurring, did not act on the information that they had to make it a matter of pubic debate. At this point, we must question White House leadership. As Clinton stated at the time, "If I do a better job of communicating our foreign policy, Americans will be much 'more understanding of what I'm trying to do."[84] At the height of the killings, Clinton was at the lowest point of public approval over his foreign policy since "the crisis in Somalia."[85] Still, two months into the killings his focus was elsewhere. In a May Los Angeles Times interview highlighting foreign policy President Clinton observed, "We've got delicate negotiations in the Middle East right now . . . and the secretary of State is involved in that and China."[86] Rwanda was apparently nowhere on the President's foreign policy radar screen.

During his first term, President Clinton showed little involvement in foreign affairs, unless they were tied to the global economic goal of enlargement. The public elected President Clinton because of his domestic skills, not his foreign policy expertise. Accordingly, he did not have the same confidence addressing foreign policy as domestic policy, nor did he have the interest.[87] The administration was also driven, more than most, by public opinion polls. Since the polling results consistently focused on domestic issues that is where he devoted his efforts. So in his first term he left foreign affairs mostly to his idealistic foreign policy team. As a result, U.S. values never came to play because the leadership and skills necessary to make it an issue were focused elsewhere.

Some of the confusion regarding what was going on in Rwanda was the result of a weak foreign policy team and an ineffective National Security Council structure. The team made up of Secretary Christopher, Secretary Perry and National Security Advisor Lake represented a party that had been out of power for 12 years and had to learn how to wield American power.[88]

Warren Christopher himself mentioned a few months before leaving office as Secretary of State, "that it had taken him some time as secretary before he fully appreciated the need for vigorous American leadership."[89]

A lack of policy coordination also troubled this first policy team. They "pretty much divided up the world according to their interest and proclivities," totally neglecting Africa and Rwanda.[90] According to a "senior U.S. governmental official who wishes to remain anonymous, 'It was clear from the beginning the JCS [Joint Chiefs of Staff] was not a willing participant. If they had their 'druthers,' they wouldn't have been involved in the effort at all.[91] Yet, somehow, in the midst of this, the administration convinced itself that the large number of deaths was the result of a brutal civil war between tribal factions—and not the result of genocide. Christopher actually refused the use of the word "genocide" for fear that it would cause the administration to "actually do something."[92]

The National Security Council was not effective in arriving at decision recommendations on the use of force. Anthony Lake, the major crisis action player, given the limited stature of Warren Christopher, had a history of not being "comfortable with exercising American power abroad."[93] Interestingly, he was also opposed the use of force in Bosnia as means to end the genocide there.[94] Lake was also uncomfortable running the National Security Council (NSC). He "became famous for chairing deliberations that never arrived at conclusions.[95] Likewise, General Collin Powell recounted in his memoirs "discussions meandered like graduate-student bull sessions or the think-tank seminars in which many of my new colleagues had spent the last twelve years while their party was out of power.[96]

Congressional action was not galvanized and grass roots support was not there to support action in Rwanda. Although the Congressional Black Caucus began sending letters to Clinton as early as May 4, 1994, urging Clinton to get the U.N. to "move," little was accomplished and little publicity came out of it.[97] The Caucus' efforts focused much more on pushing the administration to solve the Haitian problem. Likewise, there was a lack of coordinated political influence by public lobby groups. Understandably, unlike Irish, English, or Jewish immigrants, African Americans have not been as successful in gaining support for their country of origin. Therefore, Rwanda had no lobby to energize the Congress.

Mass Media

The media did not inform or influence public opinion on the Rwanda genocide because of how it was reported and because civil wars do not affect people the way lines of refugees do.[98] At first the media did not have the story straight and were in fact reporting the deaths resulted from a brutal civil war, and not from genocide. Lindsey Hilsum, a BBC reporter in Kigali during the genocide, made this point: She reflects on the "few 'facts' which I relayed to the BBC and which later turned out (as is sometimes the way with facts reported from places of terror and confusion) to be not quite true."[99] In general, this confusion persisted until a month after most of the killings had occurred, then the word "genocide" began to appear in national newspapers and newsmagazines.[100]

Even so, news of genocide did not get out quickly. In congressional testimony, Alain Detexhe, President of the International Crisis Group stated, "I strongly believe that that if General Dallaire's cable [January 1994] had been published on the front page of the New York Times or Washington Post, the genocide could have been avoided."[101] Dallaire sent the cable to the U.N. headquarters in New York three months before the genocide started, and it is widely accepted that the U.S. government had access to the information. Absent credible reporting by news organizations, "skepticism can also be deployed by governments as a convenient justification for doing nothing," as might have been the case with Rwanda.[102]

Television, the most immediate and evocative medium, initially had trouble reporting the story to the world. Given the limited number of western reporters in Rwanda at the outbreak of the genocide, television coverage was difficult at best. Finding and reporting the genocidal killings that were undeniably taking place was unsafe. "One of the very legitimate and understandable reasons so little coverage was given to the massacres in Rwanda prior to the Goma refugee coverage was the inability of journalists to move about safely in Rwanda" during the genocide.[103] It was simply too dangerous. Even when the media provided coverage of a civil war, no matter how brutal, "they simply do not have the same effect as those lines of refugees or malnourished children at a feeding station."[104] The later images, mostly of the cholera outbreak in Goma depicting suffering civilians and refugees, centered under poor conditions. They did draw a U.S. humanitarian response. Still, this reporting focused on the human tragedy of cholera and missed the political realties that brought on the cholera suffering in the first place. The mass media simply was too wrong, too little, and too late to inform public opinion or to elicit political pressure for intervention.

Policy Inertia

Policy inertia obstructed a U.S. response for two fundamental reasons. First, President Clinton's relative inattention to foreign policy, and secondly a PDD designed to reform U.S. participation in multilateral peace operations. In his first years as president, Clinton did not put much emphasis on foreign policy. Having just won the election over Gulf War hero George

16

Bush, President Clinton understood very well that domestic economics, not foreign policy, was the key to elections. Therefore, Clinton entered office expecting and pledging to "focus 'like a laser beam on the economy.' And as President elect, he stated that he might have to spend all his time on foreign policy and he did not want that to happen."[105] "Personnel at the NSC, DOS [Department of State], and DOD [Department of Defense] understood early on that their task, as much as anything, was to keep foreign policy issues from distracting the President from some of his domestic initiatives and otherwise sapping his time."[106] This internal policy prevailed and Clinton left foreign affairs to the aforementioned team. The result was that by May 1994, Clinton had become "frustrated by what he called the 'relentless criticism' of his foreign policy," about which he initially cared little, but which was beginning to threaten his reelection chances.[107]

As we have seen, Clinton's foreign policy was set mostly in administration speeches and PDDs, which were later incorporated into the 1994 NSSR. Lake gave one such speech in September 1993. In it, he made the case for limited military intervention after applying criteria such as "cost, feasibility, the permanence of the improvement our assistance will bring" and "the willingness of regional and international bodies to do their part."[108] According to Lake, "while there will be increasing calls for us to help stem bloodshed and suffering in ethnic conflicts, and while we will always bring our diplomacy to bear, these criteria suggest there will be relatively few intra-national ethnic conflicts that justify our military intervention."[109] On 3 May 1994, President Clinton signed PDD 25 thereby establishing U.S. policy on reforming peace operations. The policy directive represented a "year-long interagency policy review [and] the first comprehensive framework for U.S. decision making on issues of peace keeping and peace enforcement suited to the realities of the post cold war period."[110] Much like Lake's speech, "Presidential Decision Directive 25 argued that the U.S. should participate in a peacekeeping operation if that operation adheres to U.S. interests, its conclusion is tied to clear objectives and realistic criteria, and the consequences of inaction are unacceptable."[111] The PDD extended the policy to U.N. peace operations by imposing the same requirements and criteria on U.N. efforts. Blindly enforcing the policy, "the Clinton administration, facing the clearest case of genocide in 50 years, responded by down playing the crisis diplomatically and impeding the effective intervention of U.N. forces to stop the killing" while severely limiting U.S. military "response to the slaughter in Rwanda."[112]

As a further distraction from Rwanda, the Haitian situation was flaring up again and the President, along with his military and foreign policy advisors, were occupied with the final stages of invasion planning. Haiti was the proverbially low-hanging fruit; it presented an early election issue that continued to nag the administration. The administration thought it could rehabilitate its foreign policy with a success there. U.S. action there attracted media support and domestic support. Indeed, the administration's concentration on Haitian policies "may have drawn our attention away from the killings in Rwanda."[113]

KOSOVO

BACKGROUND

From ancient Greece and Rome through the Byzantine and Ottomans empires and two World Wars, the Balkans have been a crossroad of international conflict that has produced no winners. The past, present and future origins of the region's conflict stem from attempts over the centuries "to make nations [of different languages, religions, ethnic origins and cultures] . . . coincidental with the geographic boundaries of a state."[114] Such is most certainly the case in Kosovo, where ethnic Albanians have lived as the majority for hundreds of years, but where Serbs claim their spiritual homeland. In the 20th century, the region remained a source of conflict: Serbian nationalism was instrumental in the beginnings of World War I, and ethnic hatred polarized the region during Nazi occupation in World War II. While Tito's tight control over Yugoslavia until his death in 1980 ensured a period of relative stability in the years following World War II, the region slipped back into ancient hatreds and conflicts soon after his death.

In simple terms, the current Kosovo crisis began with the breakup of the Federal Republic of Yugoslavia and was exacerbated former Serbian President Slobodan Milosevic's policy of cleansing the region of its Muslims. In a fiery 1989 speech, he kicked off a campaign of ethnic cleansing. Hundreds of thousands of his followers listened as he promoted renewed Serbian nationalism on the "Field of Blackbirds." Defeated there by Muslims, some six hundred years earlier, the Christian Serbs vowed to return to Kosovo. Arousing historical hatreds, Milosevic invoked Serbia's spiritual and emotional claims to Kosovo as a means to strengthen his power and a reason to push the Muslims outside the boundaries of the former Yugoslavia.

Later in 1989, Milosevic followed through with his aims and abolished the autonomous status of the Kosovo region – placing it under Belgrade's direct control. His government "replaced ethnic Albanians with Serbs in most jobs, enabled Serb-owned firms to take over Albanian-owned companies, and forbade Albanians from purchasing or improving property.[115] Reacting, ethnic Albanians declared the Kosovo region a republic, established a provincial assembly, and began to combat Belgrade both nonviolently and militarily. In peaceful confrontation, they provided their own public services including education and health, by setting up "parallel, unofficial Albanian structures" using "local taxes" and contributions from Albanians outside the province.[116] The Kosovo Liberation Army (KLA), supported by unrest in neighboring Albania, began to attack Serbian police and Yugoslav military forces. Initially seen as armed bandits by both NATO and Belgrade, the KLA came to represent the Kosovars within the region and internationally through a number of skillful political and military moves.

The conflict in the Balkans escalated through much of the 1990s, fueled by a systematic ethnic cleansing effort on Milosevic's part. The U.N. responded to Milosevic's efforts in Bosnia with a weak U.N. peacekeeping operation that ultimately succeeded through support of NATO air strikes and a NATO led stabilization force. But the conflict soon spread to Kosovo. In 1996, the KLA initiated reprisals for continued oppression from Belgrade and against attacks by Serbian police forces on ethnic Albanians. Fearing the spread of violence and a Bosnia-like humanitarian catastrophe, the international community, including the United Nations, NATO, and the European Union (E.U.), began to seek solutions to the growing conflict. In March 1998, The U.N. Security Council condemned the "excessive use of force by Serbian police against Kosovar civilians" by adopting UNR 1160.[117] During 1998, conflict between the Serbian military and police forces and Kosovar Albanian forces produced over 1,500 Kosovar Albanians killed and forced 400,000 to flee from their homes.[118] This slaughter and displacement led to UNR 1199, demanding "a cessation of hostilities" and a warning that the U.N. would consider "additional measures to maintain or restore peace and stability in the regions" if Belgrade did not comply.[119] In October, threats of NATO air strikes forced Milosevic to withdraw forces from Kosovo, end the violence, and support the return of refugees. Meanwhile the Organization for Security and Cooperation in Europe (OSCE) established the Kosovo Verification Mission (KVM) to ensure Milosevic's compliance. Then NATO began aerial surveillance for the same reason. The U.N. endorsed both missions through adoption of UNR 1203.[120]

In 1999, the Kosovo crisis came to a head. The bodies of 45 ethnic Albanians were discovered in Racak. Ambassador Richard Walker, the KVM Chief for OSCE , in a much publicized news conference attributed the massacre to Serbian forces. The massacre and resulting news coverage galvanized U.S. Secretary of State Madeline Albright and NATO allies to act. During February and March of 1999, the six-nation Contact Group (United States, Britain, France, Germany, Italy and Russia) and three co-mediators representing the U.S., the E.U., and the Russian Federation attempted to gain a peaceful resolution to the conflict. The February talks broke down when the Kosovars refused to sign the agreement because it failed to provide for the autonomy of Kosovo. By the time the talks were reconvened in March, the KLA representatives, under pressure, were ready to sign a similar document. This time, however, the Serbs objected to any provision for a NATO-led force in Kosovo and walked out.

19

Meanwhile, Serb forces launched a previously planned military/cleansing operation in Kosovo, killing hundreds, burning houses, and forcing thousands of Kosovar Albanians to flee to neighboring Albania and Montenegro.[121]

On 24 March 1999, after international initiatives, U.N. resolutions, short-lived Serbian promises, and diplomacy failed to resolve the situation peacefully, NATO undertook military operations to force Milosevic to comply with the international community's demands. On 10 June 1999, following an eleven-week NATO air campaign, Milosevic agreed to NATO and Contact Group principles outlining a political solution that eventually became part of UNR 1244. This resolution continues to provide the international community with a broad "mandate to establish democratic self-governing institutions to ensure conditions for a peaceful normal life for all inhabitants of Kosovo."[122]

FACTORS INVOLVED IN THE KOSOVO INTERVENTION.

Ideology

Several ideological factors lead the administration to intervene in Kosovo. Among them was a willingness to rely on regional alliances rather than multilateral U.N. action, as well as greater reliance on the dictates of realism. While multilateralism, as represented by the U.N., remained a central theme of administration's rhetoric, the administration's actions regarding military force and economic policy were not truly multilateral. The administration continued to discover that assertive multilateralism was "more complicated in practice than principle."[123] This is particularly true of multilateral peace operations, in which collective decision-making could "limit U.S. options and block decisive actions."[124] Somalia, Rwanda, Haiti and Bosnia all provided lessons concerning the role of the military in foreign policy and reliance on the U.N. in conducting that policy. Eventually, the administration developed a more pragmatic view of multilateralism, "encapsulated in the mantra, 'multilateral when we can, unilateral when we must.'"[125]

According to the administration, U.S. involvement in Kosovo resulted from the "nexus of our national values and interests."[126] Although his idealism was still prevalent, President Clinton showed a greater reliance on realist ideology than in his earlier decisions. In March 1999, Clinton's speech to the American people revealed both an idealist and a realist rationale for U.S. intervention: "Ending this tragedy [in Kosovo] is a moral imperative. It is also important to America's national interest."[127] As former President Jimmy Carter lamented in a 1999 New York Times op-ed piece, "The approach the U.S. has taken recently has been to devise a solution

20

that best suits it own purposes, recruit at least tacit support in whichever forum it can best influence, provide the dominant military force, present an ultimatum to recalcitrant parties and then take punitive action . . . to force compliance."[128] Acting in its interests and fearing Security Council vetoes, from either China or Russia would limit its actions and options, the administration circumvented the Council and used its leadership in NATO to drive policy toward intervention in Kosovo.

Global Systems

The Balkans played a role in almost every confrontation among world powers in the twentieth century. Trying to avoid mistakes made in Bosnia and recognizing the potential of increased conflict in the region, the administration committed itself to action in Kosovo but faced the realties of global politics. United States relations within the U.N. and with NATO were key factors influencing the administration's decisions and its ability to intervene in Kosovo; U.S. relations with Russia and China prevented it from operating within the U.N., while NATO relevance and credibility were both perceived to be on the line in Kosovo.

The U.N., the organization that could provide the administration's efforts with the most legitimacy, was nonetheless an obstacle to achieving peace in Kosovo. Russia, a historical Serbian ally, with strong ethnic, economic, military and political ties to the Serbs, would not support military intervention in Kosovo. It viewed Kosovo as a slippery slope, especially given its own ethnic conflict in Chechnya. Russian also saw intervention in Kosovo as a threat to its regional influence, particularly at a time when NATO was looking to expand eastward. Not wanting to threaten Russia, the administration attempted to find a middle ground, one that recognized Russia's lessening powers but did so without embarrassing it about its own conflict. Another reason for remaining engaged with the Russians was to ensure their continued role as an intermediary between Belgrade and NATO. Chinese views were similar to the Russians' on Kosovo: They regarded the matter as strictly an internal affair of Belgrade. The administration also had to take into account U.S. economic interests in China if it was to achieve their support. Therefore, any efforts to use the U.N. for legitimacy also risked a veto on the Security Council. To avoid a direct political confrontation with both countries, the administration turned to NATO as a surrogate to achieve multilateral credibility.

The Kosovo crisis was occurring about the time NATO was celebrating it 50th Anniversary. Given the post-Cold War environment, NATO was looking for a continued purpose. Kosovo followed the relative success in Bosnia, where NATO employed ground troops with little loss of life. However, despite that success, NATO risked becoming irrelevant. So Kosovo gave it a reason to be. The administration argued that ethnic cleansing challenged our national values, while stability in Europe was vital to our own national security. Therefore, U.S. military forces committed to NATO, served to protect U.S. interests in Europe. Since the administration declared "European stability vital to U.S. security," it was fighting hard to change the organization from one dedicated to common defense to a "crucial element of the U.S. and Allied strategy to build an undivided, peaceful Europe."[129] Continued NATO relevance was thus instrumental to the administration's strategy of engagement and commitment to Europe.

While relevance was one issue, directly related was NATO's credibility. NATO had "threatened military action so many times that its credibility was at stake" if it and its lead country did not intervene.[130] General Wesley Clark, Supreme Allied Commander, Europe, went as far as to say that if NATO did not succeed in Kosovo it "could likely not have survived in its present form".[131] Moreover, he "warned that a NATO failure would bring the collapse of several European governments, as well."[132]

Public and Elite convictions

Whereas public and Congressional convictions had little to do with U.S. involvement in Kosovo, elite convictions had much to do with it. Congress, interest groups and the public remained divided over the question of U.S. involvement, but Secretary of State Madeline Albright was committed to resolving the crisis in the Balkans. In addition, President Clinton became more involved in the execution of foreign policy as world events lessened his singular focus on domestic policy.

As U.S. Ambassador to the U.N., Madeline Albright took a strong, early stand against Serbian aggression in Bosnia; as Secretary of State, she wanted to avoid inaction in Kosovo. In a Time article entitled "Madeline's War," Walter Isaacson pointed out that "more than anyone else," Madeline Albright embodied "the foreign policy vision that pushed . . . war."[133] Albright is very much the product of her immigrant background. She was actually in Munich when Chamberlain traded Czechoslovakia to the Nazis. For example, in a 1998 meeting with allied leaders, "Italian and French foreign ministers proposed a softening in the language they would use to threaten the Serbs. Albright's close aide Jamie Rubin whispered to her that she could probably accept it. She snapped back, 'Where do you think we are, Munich?'"[134]

Secretary Albright was an interventionist known for publicly voicing her strong convictions. Some say that she won the secretary of state "job with her savvy political skills and her hawkish sound bites – especially her, 'This is not cojones, this is cowardice' poke at Castro.'"[135] Her challenge, made in private, to the Chairman of the Joint Chiefs of Staff, General Powell asking

"What's the point of having this superb military" if it wasn't to be used was another sound bite that garnered her some support.[136] In another interview she explained, "We get involved where the crime is huge, where it's in a region that affects our stability – the stability of Europe is something that has been essential to the U.S. for the last 200 years – and where there is an organization capable of dealing with it. Just because you can't act everywhere doesn't mean you don't act anywhere."[137] Her mission, she told to a <u>Washington Post</u> reporter, was "to rescue U.S. military might from the clutches of the Powell Doctrine" – a doctrine that required U.S. interests, overwhelming force, a clear purpose and exit strategy.[138]

Critics often accused Albright of "getting out ahead of Clinton on rhetoric [and] close associates say that her MO [modus operandi] was often to shove policy along in her direction by laying out aggressive markers for the endlessly equivocating Clinton to follow."[139] On Kosovo, according to one aide, she made a conscious decision in March 1998 to lead through her rhetoric.[140] Indeed, Albright's deep-rooted convictions and force of personality drove the U.S. and its NATO allies to action in Kosovo. According to Albright, the U.S. was not "going to stand by and watch Serbian authorities do in Kosovo what they can no longer get away with doing in Bosnia."[141] However, in the same breath she did acknowledge that there were some shortcomings. "We're evolving these rules [U.S. involvement in Kosovo]. There's not a doctrine that really sets this forth in an organized way yet."[142] Because of her position on the use of force, known as coercive diplomacy, she was linked to the war's largest controversy. The administration, with Madeline Albright in the lead, badly underestimated Milosevic's resolve and found itself caught off guard, politically and militarily, when NATO bombing led Milosevic to accelerate his ethnic cleansing of Kosovar Albanians.

Perhaps goaded by Secretary Albright's outspoken activism, Clinton displayed a greater interest in foreign policy for a number of reasons. As Robert Kagan observed, "If you are the president of the United States, somehow foreign policy finds you."[143] Somalia, Haiti and Bosnia all required that the president rethink the approach to foreign policy that he initially brought into the oval office. Another was Clinton's increasingly close ties to Tony Blair. Blair's "sincere" desire to achieve peace in the Balkans was a contributing factor in Clinton's commitment to our involvement in Kosovo.[144] A third reason resided in domestic politics: NATO expansion was viewed as a "prime enticement to critical swing voters . . . particularly Polish-American voters," so Clinton made "geopolitics a subset of his geo-economic strategy."[145] A domestic commitment to NATO required the President to support its relevance and continued credibility overseas. Likewise, the administration's lack of action in Rwanda and its late response in

Bosnia jeopardized Presidents Clinton's overall humanitarian record. To ensure his legacy, he had to take decisive action in Kosovo. Lastly, Kosovo simply provided an escape mechanism. Foreign policy permitted Clinton to redirect a number of questions concerning his personal record. Nevertheless, his increased involvement did not alleviate his fundamental unease about using military force. Faced with this unease concerning "military force and wanting to achieve military and political goals overseas without losing votes at home," he handled Kosovo as a low-threat action. He authorized precision air strikes, but no ground troops to ensure low risk of U.S. combat casualties.[146]

Congressional support was divided. The Senate gave tepid support to Clinton's Kosovo policy with a 58 to 41 vote-authorizing air strikes against Serbia.[147] However, many senators say that support came only after Clinton made a personal appeal before the vote.[148] While the resolution did not have the force of law, the symbolic support of the Senate was crucial for the White House, since Republicans had control of the Senate at the time. By contrast, during the air war the House failed, in a 213 to 213 vote, to support air strikes against Serbia.[149]

Public opinion, reflecting the closeness of both the Senate and House votes, was slightly less in favor of operations in Kosovo. Pre-war polling data compiled by the American Enterprise Institute showed that the number of Americans who thought Kosovo involved a vital U.S. interest remained fewer than 42 percent. Likewise, on the question of whether the U.S. needed to be involved to protect its own interests, the highest prewar poll data showed only 43 percent. However, on 25 March, 64 percent of respondents to a Gallup/CNN/USA Today poll said that the U.S. had a "moral obligation to help keep peace in Kosovo."[150] In May, both polls showed U.S. support for the use of ground troops in Kosovo to be less than 50 percent.[151]

Leaders inspire public confidence and shape public opinion by their presence and words. In part, the lack of public support for U.S. intervention in Kosovo may be attributed to the Clinton impeachment process. As the ambassador of a close U.S. ally said of the situation, "You'd have to be deaf, dumb and a mental defective not see that Clinton has been weakened in his capacity to lead, at home and abroad."[152] The media's focus on a sex scandal and President Clinton's resulting unwillingness to get out and publicly make the case for Kosovo, before the end of the Senate impeachment trial probably distracted from public support for intervention.

Groups opposing U.S. action in Kosovo had little effect. For example, while Jessie Jackson highlighted a concern among many African-Americans that the U.S. undermined its humanitarian credibility in Kosovo by not acting elsewhere in the world, most notably in Sierra Leone, little came of it. Jackson argued that 500,000 lives were lost and more than a million people were displaced "outside the glare of cameras and beyond the eyes of Western journalists."[153] But his attempt to garner media attention, the same group he was railing against, was weakened by the news of the day: Clinton's ongoing sexual misconduct scandal.

Mass Media

There is no indication that the media had a significant impact on the willingness of Americans to go to war, one way or the other. The media kept Kosovo in the headlines mostly through policy debates and NATO threats; nonetheless, public opinion remained pretty much split. There were several reasons the media had little impact, primarily lack of access and credibility. In a situation similar to that in Rwanda, correspondents reporting Kosovo before the war did so at their own peril. "Crossing into the terror zone for proof of gang rape, mass execution and medieval torture, the worst in Europe since the Nazi era, could be fodder for a Pulitzer Prize. It could also be a death sentence." A veteran stringer for U.S. New and World Report was ordered out of Kosovo and his passport stamped "permanently invalid," and a state-run newspaper branded him the "the Balkan bureau chief for the CIA."[154] Without reliable access, the media relied on sterile governmental reports that were difficult to verify. More importantly, no grisly photographs were available to influence public opinion. Television needs lots of action to be successful. As Chief NATO Spokesman Jamie P. Shea declared, "No pictures, no news."[155] According to Shea, "the advantage of television over newspapers is that we [NATO] write the script and millions more listen to it than is the case with newspapers."[156]

One of the exceptions to this limited media impact was the January 1999 discovery of 45 dead ethnic Albanians in the village of Racavak, which made front-page news. According to Albright, this story prodded the administration to act. A Washington Post article that reconstructed the Kosovo decision-making process stated, "Racak transformed the West's Balkan policy as singular events seldom do."[157] Very graphic photos and the credibility of Ambassador Walker, the source, were critical elements in the story's ability to influence the administration and its NATO allies.

Policy Inertia

Policy inertia played a part in both the administration's rationale to go to war and the U.S. ability or willingness to do so. That is, a stable Europe and NATO credibility provided the rationale for going to war, where casualty avoidance dictated the means as an air war. The fundamental policy inertia in play during the Kosovo crisis regarded our commitment to a stable Europe. As Madeline Albright explained, "the crisis in the southern Serb province affects U.S. interests. American soldiers in huge numbers have been drawn to Europe to fight wars that either began in the Balkans or that sparked bitter fighting there."[158] Likewise, our commitment to Europe over the last fifty years obligated us to respond. Albright also claimed our withdrawal from Europe after World War I meant that "an entire generation of brave Europeans and American paid the price" for U.S. isolationism. [159] Knowing we had invested so much in Bosnia and with NATO credibility on the line, the administration concluded it was forced to do something in Kosovo for fear of losing what we had already gained. Aware "that renewed violence in Kosovo could seriously jeopardize Bosnia's progress toward peace," the President concluded that past efforts in Europe and Bosnia made Kosovo a must do. [160] This rationale was similar to the Dean Rusk argument "that South Vietnam had become a vital U.S. interest because we had sunk so much foreign aid into it."[161] Given the unparalleled growth in European economic unity during the 1990s, concerns about European stability may have been exaggerated.

Additionally, within the administration a casualty aversion policy contributed to inertia. While this policy certainly did not drive the U.S. to intervene, it created conditions that made military intervention more palatable within the administration and to the public, given the lack of a clearly articulated national interest. Until the end of the crisis, it also influenced the manner in which NATO conducted air operations. The limited application of force policy stemmed from fear of casualties, a fallout from Somalia. "They [the administration] believe that Somalia demonstrates conclusively that you cannot have any casualties . . . . They take this as a matter of faith."[162] The administration used the threat of air attack because precedent indicated Milosevic would back down; further it was a low risk, antiseptic option. NATO air strikes had prompted Milosevic to agree to the Dayton Accords in 1995 and in 1998 when the threat of NATO air attacks caused Belgrade to agree to a ceasefire. The White House therefore assumed that Milosevic would respond any new bombing in the same way. A supporting argument was that Milosevic could use NATO airpower as a public excuse to walk away from Kosovo without losing face. But the administration underestimated the symbolic importance of Kosovo to Serbia and Milosevic's resolve to retain it. Also, there was no effort to think through alternatives to the incremental use of force.

The administration was so certain of the strategy that it ignored any alternative, to include the use of ground troops. According to General George A. Joulwan, a former Supreme Allied Commander, Europe, "We might have been seduced a little by technology rather than by good professional judgment of what is necessary to win a war."[163] Similarly, when asked by the visiting Italian prime minister what would happen if bombing alone did not force Belgrade to back down, "President Clinton was reportedly unprepared to answer . . . after a brief hesitation .

. . Berger responded: We will continue the bombing."[164] Many consider the lack of a credible ground force as one of the major reasons that Milosevic persisted in his policy of ethnic cleansing.

CRISES COMPARISON

IDEOLOGY

Similar ideologies influenced the administration during both the Rwandan and Kosovo crises. By the time the Rwandan genocide occurred the administration had already begun to shift to a less multilateral and idealist approach to foreign policy. This shift resulted from its early lessons in Bosnia, Haiti, and – most importantly – Somalia. The 1994 NSSR and PDD 25 both reveal this shift from Clinton's earlier views. After the 1994 NSSR, "President Clinton offered no new broad overview of strategic security policy."[165] What did occur between the 1994 NSSR and Kosovo in 1999 was a clearer articulation of U.S. interests and criteria for the use of force in protecting those interests, something that neither the 1994 NSSR nor PDD 25 provided.

The primary difference between Rwanda and Kosovo was not so much in ideology but in a paralysis of ideology in the administration during the Rwandan crisis. No such paralysis inhibited Kosovo decisions. However, some analysts may point less at a paralysis of ideology and more at a titanic shift toward pragmatism, given the administration's argument that it initially viewed the Rwanda crisis as a civil war and not genocide. Although, that argument weakens when you look at the ideological bent of the foreign policy team and President Clinton's lack of attention to foreign policy at the time. The evidence indicates Clinton's inaction was based on the political fear of another Somalia or USS Harlan County episode.[166] The political damage was so great from Somalia that "as few risks as possible were to be taken and certainly none in Africa."[167] One would certainly assume that, absent Somalia, the administration's idealistic bent would have driven it to action had Clinton not been so concerned with polls. The U.S. action in Kosovo was based on a mixture of Wilsonian idealism and realism. President Clinton articulated this point when he observed, U.S. involvement in Kosovo resulted from the "nexus of our national values and interests."[168]

GLOBAL SYSTEMS

From the perspective of global systems, three significant observations: First, the question of U.S. interests was very much at the heart of each crisis. Second, there was a great disparity in regional alliances. Third, Russia and the U.N. played very different roles in the two crises.

The U.S. has never given Africa the same level focus that it has given to Europe. Comments by Secretary Albright's make this point clear: "We get involved where the crime is huge, where it's in a region that affects our stability – the stability of Europe is something that has been essential to the U.S. for the last 200 years – and where there is an organization capable of dealing with it. Just because you can't act every where doesn't mean you don't act anywhere."[169] Even at the height of our interest in Africa during the Cold War, Africa was merely a means to contain Soviet expansion that threatened a fundamental interest in Europe.

Regional alliances played a role both the Rwanda and Kosovo crises, but they differed in capabilities and levels of success. The OAU was of limited value in stopping the Rwandan civil war and controlling the ethnic violence that ravaged Rwanda in the early 1960s. Given its political and economic, rather than military focus it offered limited military and logistical capabilities and relied heavily on outside forces like the U.N. and former colonial powers to assist it in accomplishing its peacekeeping goals. The diversity of the organization was also a limiting factor given the ethnic nature of the conflict. Conversely, there was a much stronger and effective regional alliance in Europe. With the U.S. as a primary contributor, NATO was better prepared to assist in accomplishing its objectives. Domestic support for NATO in the U.S. was also a factor in its ability to act, something obviously absent for the OAU. Some voters in the U.S. saw NATO expansion as a source of ethnic pride as it expanded and became engaged in humanitarian operations. For all its faults, NATO mustered forces under U.S. leadership and acted to intervene with a coordinated stand. The same cannot be said of the U.S., French, Belgian and OAU efforts in Rwanda.

In a sense, the U.N. was an important supporting player in both Rwanda and Kosovo but for different reasons. In the case of Rwanda, it enabled the U.S. to avoid a meaningful intervention. But in the case of Kosovo, it forced the U.S. to take on the challenge "unilaterally" through NATO. The U.N. was susceptible to the U.S. inclination not to intervene in Rwanda for several reasons. One was obviously U.S. veto power. Another was that the U.S. was an obvious supplier of military capabilities necessary to conduct a speedy intervention, so the U.N. could not effectively intervene without U.S. support. A third was that the U.N. was also negatively affected by the fallout of its operation in Somalia and did not welcome another unclear mandate. Conversely, given the threat of Security Council vetoes in the U.N. by other countries and its inability to enforce the Bosnian peace process, the U.N. tacitly deferred to U.S. uses of NATO in Kosovo. With Kosovo, the primary probability of veto came from the Russians, a historic ally of Serbia; Russians saw their own conflict in Chechnya as the next place for U.N.

28

intervention if they supported a U.N. intervention in Kosovo. NATO provided the U.S. with a convenient fallback position for support in Kosovo.

PUBLIC AND ELITE CONVICTIONS

Evaluation of similarities and differences of public and elite convictions provides three observations: First, there were significant differences between the tendencies and ideologies of President Clinton's first foreign policy team and his second that were not necessarily revealed in published NSSRs. Secondly, in neither case was there a ground swell of public or congressional support for the administration to intervene. Lastly, while the President was more engaged in policy matters involving Kosovo than Rwanda, in neither case was the President's conviction an important factor in intervention.

There were significant differences between the Rwandan foreign policy team and the Kosovo team. The fundamental difference was in their willingness to act. A source of this difference was their levels of experience. Both the National Security Advisor Sandy Berger and Secretary of State Madeline Albright had several years under their belts when they assumed their second, and more important, jobs within the administration. Both had become attuned to ways and means to exercise national power through their experience, more so than their predecessors had.

Secretary Albright also brought with her a strong sense of conviction concerning Kosovo. The same level of conviction was not evident in the Rwanda crisis. These convictions were shaped in part by her experience in the U.N. dealing with Bosnia and her personal background. As the U.S. Ambassador to the U.N., Madeline Albright took a strong early stand against Serbian aggression in Bosnia, and as Secretary of State she wanted to avoid inaction in Kosovo. She was passionate in her objections to Milosevic and his ethnic cleansing policies because of her own family's exodus experience.[170] Her vocal position and out-front comments demonstrated her convictions. As _Time_ pointed out "more than anyone else," Madeline Albright embodied "the foreign policy vision that pushed . . . war."[171] Conversely, no one spoke out for African policy in the first administration. As noted, the first team "pretty much divided up the world according to their interest and proclivities," apparently leaving Africa and Rwanda out.[172] When the genocide began, instead of seeking ways to react the administration sought ways not to.

In neither case was there strong public or congressional pressure to intervene. In the case of Rwanda, initial inaccurate and unavailable media coverage prevented a clear mobilization of public opinion. As mentioned, absent credible reporting by news organizations,

29

governments can use skepticism as a "convenient justification for doing nothing," which might have been the case with in Rwanda.[173] In the case of Kosovo, Congressional and public opinion remained split. The only significant Congressional support was a 424 to 1 House vote backing the military personnel conducting the war.[174]

In neither case did Presidential conviction seem to matter. In the case of Rwanda, assuming that he was not aware of the genocide until when U.S. media began reporting it around 25 April, it was then too late to stop most of the killings: Further, President Clinton delegated the process and focus of foreign policy to others in the administration. If he and his administration were aware that genocide was going to occur, as warnings indicated, they remained too paralyzed by their experience in Somalia to act. While there was a greater emphasis on foreign policy by the President up to Kosovo, any convictions the President had, on Kosovo, were muted by involvement in a personal scandal. It was not until 19 March 1999, following his acquittal in the Senate impeachment trial, that he held his first press conference in nine months.[175]

MASS MEDIA

In neither case did the media drive public opinion toward intervention. Except for Racavak, the media had limited influence on policy decisions. Several reasons account for the lack of media influence on public opinion. In both cases, physical challenges over reporting the crisis prevented an accurate portrayal of what was occurring. The personal safety of reporters and media access were factors in both Rwanda and Kosovo. This "news blackout" is nothing new. Personal safety issues in Somalia left Mogadishu with few reporters after Somali clan members killed several reporters in 1993. The initial misunderstanding of what was occurring in Rwanda affected public perception and opinion. As stated earlier, coverage of civil wars has less of an impact than refugee coverage while repeated coverage of atrocities can sometimes have desensitizing effect on the public. Regarding the Racavak story, in Secretary Albright's view it was a defining moment that goaded the administration to action. The credibility of the source and the graphic nature of the accompanying photos increased its effect. There was no such crystallizing moment within the administration during the Rwandan genocide.

POLICY INERTIA

Policy inertia was an important contributing factor to inaction in Rwanda and intervention in Kosovo. A policy bred out of failure in Somalia provided inertia for the U.S. to remain uninvolved in Rwanda. Likewise, an informal policy within the administration left the President uninvolved. While the purpose of PDD 25 was to limit U.S. participation in peace operations to those that furthered U.S. interests, it did not define those interests. That task remained the purview of the President, but absent guidance to the contrary a crisis remained outside the scope of U.S. interest. While it seems far-fetched that a President could find himself in a situation where he is out of the loop on important foreign policy matters, it does happen. When the USS Harlan County was turned back from Port au Prince in October 1993, President Clinton "was furious and blamed his NSC staff for putting him in a lose-lose situation.[176]

A much broader policy inertia affected the Kosovo intervention. The fundamental policy inertia leading to Kosovo was the U.S. commitment to a stable Europe. That policy was supported by several others who feared losing what was gained in Europe over a period of 50 years and what was recently gained by our recent presence in Bosnia. Our policy involving U.S. intervention in Kosovo was also linked to a policy of casualty avoidance that restricted the war's prosecution solely to air attacks. While the policy of casualty avoidance allowed NATO to prosecute the air war, no such alternative was available in Rwanda. In Rwanda, low risk, low cost air power would not have made a difference.

CONCLUSION

The foregoing analysis points to several factors showing why the U.S. did not intervene to stop genocide in Rwanda, but did intervene in Kosovo. Ideology generally influenced the U.S. response to events in Kosovo, but failed to affect U.S. actions toward Rwanda. While President Clinton's ideological inclinations would indicate some sort of response in Rwanda, he was unwilling to risk intervention because of the political threat he faced following the administration's sobering experience in Somalia. A pragmatic/realist approach allowed the administration to intervene in Kosovo without much public or congressional support for the operation. By the time of Kosovo crisis, ideological penchants in the White House had shifted to the pragmatic domain, if not the realist one. This shift occurred for two reasons: First, the second term election brought a more pragmatic foreign policy team to the administration. Second, President Clinton was more involved in foreign policy decisions and had learned lessons in Somali, Haiti, Rwanda, and Bosnia on the U.N. and use of force. The lessons of Haiti and Bosnia revealed that force, or threat of it, could be employed with little political risk if the size and means of force could be constrained and the U.N. was marginalized. In part, intervention in Kosovo was practicable because of its low cost, low-risk, and unilateral nature.

Convictions played a significant role leading to U.S. intervention in Kosovo. It was Secretary Albright's fervor was most important to intervention. The President's withdrawal from public debate over Kosovo, because of his personal misconduct challenges, facilitated

Secretary Albright's ability to publicly promote her position. There were no strong convictions in the White House or State Department during Rwanda. At the time, President Clinton was relying on a relatively inexperienced and cautious team, led by Anthony Lake and Warren Christopher, while Clinton concentrated exclusively on domestic issues. This foreign policy team was most reluctant to use military force.

Global systems were also a significant factor contributing to inaction in Rwanda and action in Kosovo. For example, the lack of a credible regional alliance or organization in Africa and the presence of one in Europe lead to very different decisions on intervention. Alliances offer a means to achieve an end. In Rwanda, as in Africa as a whole, there was no significant U.S. national interest or end to meet. President Clinton revealed as much in his 1994 NSSR, which admitted "Africa is one of our greatest challenges for a strategy of engagement and enlargement."[177] Conversely, our involvement in Kosovo provided a way to demonstrate U.S. commitment to the relevance and credibility of NATO and ensure a U.S. end, a stable and secure Europe.

The "CNN factor" was not a factor. In neither case was the mass media a major contributor to U.S. action or inaction. While the media has the capability to influence policy, as Racavak did, the media's coverage of events before and during the two crises failed to significantly change public opinion. In Rwanda, the media's role might have been different had the media correctly reported that genocide was occurring before it was too late. However, given the lack of public support for operations in Kosovo, even when provided with factual data on ethnic cleansing in Kosovo, we cannot assume that accurate media coverage alone would have resulted in any change of public opinion to intervene there. This was in part because the experience of Somalia had undermined public support for humanitarian operations.

Finally, in both Rwanda and Kosovo, policy inertia affected the U.S. response. In the case of Rwanda, it prevented a timely and effective U.S. action. The administration rationalized inaction in Rwanda based on the intent of PDD 25 and the degree to which President Clinton was uninvolved in foreign policy. With Kosovo, policy inertia provided a basis for intervention and indeed dictated the means by which the intervention was carried out. Our historical commitment to Europe and the administration's desire to ensure that nothing gained in Bosnia was lost through conflict spread into Kosovo maintained this inertia.

WORD COUNT = 14,238

ENDNOTES

[1]Congressional Research Service, 'Instances of Unites States Forces Abroad. 1798-1993 (Washington, D.C.: Congressional Research Service, October 1993) available from < http://www.history.navy.mil/wars/foabroad.htm>; Internet; accessed 24 November 2002.

[2]Robert H. Dorf, "Some Basic Concepts and Approaches to the Study of International Politics," in U.S. Army War College Guide to Strategy, ed. Joseph R. Cerami and James F. Holcomb Jr., (Carlisle Barracks, PA: Strategic Studies Institute, U.S. Army War College, 2001), 31.

[3]Don M. Snider and John A. Nagel, "The National Security Strategy: Documenting a Vision," in U.S. Army War College Guide to Strategy, ed. Joseph R. Cerami and James F. Holcomb Jr., (Carlisle Barracks, PA: Strategic Studies Institute, U.S. Army War College, 2001), 127.

[4]Michael G. Roskin. "National Interest: From Abstraction to Strategy." in U.S. Army War College Guide to Strategy, ed. Joseph R. Cerami and James F. Holcomb Jr., (Carlisle Barracks, PA: Strategic Studies Institute, U.S. Army War College, 2001), 62-65.

[5]Donald E. Neuchterlein, "Defining U.S. National Interests: An Analytical Framework," America Overcommitted: United States National Interests in the 1980s. University of Kentucky Press, Lexington, KY, excerpt reprinted in U.S. Army War College, Course 2: "War, National Security Policy & Strategy Readings Vol I, (Carlisle Barracks, PA.. 30 July 2002), 312.

[6]Roskin, 56.

[7]Ibid.

[8]Ibid.

[9]Ibid.

[10]Neuchterlein, 309.

[11]Snider, Don M. and Nagel, John A. "The National Security Strategy: Documenting a Vision." In U.S. Army War College Guide to Strategy, ed. Joseph R. Cerami and James F. Holcomb Jr., 127-142. Carlisle Barracks, PA: Strategic Studies Institute, U.S. Army War College, 2001.130-131.

[12]Ibid., 129.

[13]Ibid., 134.

[14]James M. McCormick, "Clinton and Foreign Policy." in The Postmodern Presidency, ed. Steven E. Schier, (Pittsburgh, PA: University of Pittsburgh Press, 2000), 62-63.

[15]Anthony Lake, "From Containment to Enlargement," lecture, John Hopkins University, School of Advanced International Studies, 21 September 1993. Available from <http://www.mtholyoke.edu/acad/intrel/lakedoc.html>; Internet; accessed 24 November 2002.

[16]William J. Clinton, <u>A National Security Strategy of Engagement and Enlargement</u>. Washington D.C. White House, July 1994. i and ii.

[17]Ibid., i and 5.

[18]Ibid.

[19]McCormick, 65.

[20]Clinton, 1994 NSSR, 6.

[21]William J.Clinton, <u>Presidential Decision Directive 25, Reforming Multilateral Peace Operations</u>, (Washington, D.C.: The White House, 6 May 1994); available from <http:/www.fas.org/irp/offdocs/pdd25.html> Internet; accessed 22 September 2002. 2

[22]Congressional Budget Office Report. <u>Making Peace While Staying Ready for War: The Challenges of U.S. Military Participation in Peace Operations</u>. (Washington, D.C.: U.S. Congressional Budget Office, December 1999); Available from <http:/www.cbo.gov/showdoc.cfm?index+1809&sequence =2>. Internet; accessed on 22 September 2002. 4.

[23]Snider, 135.

[24]McCormick, 64.

[25]Rubinstein, Alvin Z., Shayevich, Albiana and Zlotnikov, Boris, eds. <u>The Clinton Foreign Policy Reader</u>. Armonk, NY. M.E. Sharpe., 2000. 7.

[26]William J. Clinton, <u>A National Security Strategy for a New Century</u> (Washington D.C.: The White House, October 1998), i.

[27]Snider, 136.

[28]Ibid.

[29]Ibid.

[30]William J. Clinton, <u>A National Security Strategy for a New Century</u>. (Washington D.C.: The White House, May 1997), ii, 21.

[31]Clinton, 1998 NSSR, 38.

[32]Roskin, 62.

[33]Ibid.

[34]Terry, L. Deibel, "Clinton and Congress: The Politics of Foreign Policy." <u>Foreign Policy Association Headline Series</u>, 321 (Fall 2000): 13.

[35] Ibid.

[36] Roskin, 64.

[37] Robert B. Oakley and David Tucker, <u>Two Perspectives on Interventions and Humanitarian Operations</u> (Strategic Studies Institute, Carlisle Barracks: U.S. Army War College, 1997), 19.

[38] Roskin, 64-65.

[39] Ibid., 64.

[40] Ibid., 64-65.

[41] Ibid., 65.

[42] Damian P. Carr, <u>U.S. Army Public Affairs During Operation Uphold Democracy</u>, Masters Thesis, (Fort Leavenworth: U.S. Army Command and General Staff College 1996), 13.

[43] Ibid., 14-5.

[44] Roskin, 65.

[45] Steven Metz, <u>Disaster and Intervention in Sub-Saharan Africa: Learning from Rwanda</u>. (Strategic Studies Institute, Carlisle Barracks: U.S. Army War College, 1994); available from <http://www.carlisle.army.mil/ssi/pubs/1994/rwanda/rwanda.htm>. Internet; accessed 24 November 2002.

[46] Ibid.

[47] Organization for African Unity, <u>Report on Rwandan Genocide, Executive Summary</u> June 2000. Provided by COL Thomas A. Dempsey, Faculty Instructor, U.S. Army War College, Carlisle Barracks, PA. 2.

[48] Metz, 3.

[49] Ibid.

[50] Organization for African; Metz, 3.

[51] Linda. Melvern, <u>A People Betrayed: The Role of the West in Rwanda's Genocide</u> (New York: Zed Books LTD, 2000), 241.

[52] Metz, 3.; Organization for African Unity, 2.

[53] Scott R. Feil, <u>Preventing Genocide: How the Early Use of Force Might Have Succeeded in Rwanda, A Report to the Carnegie Commission on Preventing Deadly Conflict</u> (New York: Carnegie Corporation, 1998), 5.

[54] Melvern, 244.

[55]Gerard Prunier, <u>The Rwanda Crisis: History of a Genocide</u> (New York: Columbia University Press, 1995), 222-223.

[56]Ibid.

[57]Ibid.

[58]Melvern, 245.

[59]Alan J. Kuperman, <u>The Limits of Humanitarian Intervention</u> (Washington, D.C.: Brookings Institution Press, 2001), 30.

[60]Ibid., 27-30.

[61]Ibid., 30.

[62]Ibid., 110.

[63]Melvern, 246.

[64]Prunier, 298.

[65]Melvern, 247.

[66]Prunier, 287-290.

[67]Ibid., 303-304.

[68]Stephen M. Walt, "Two Cheers for Clinton's Foreign Policy," <u>Foreign Affairs,</u> 79 # 2 (March/April 2000); available from <http://www.foreignpolicy2000.org/library/issuebriefs/readingnotes/fa_walt.html>; Internet; accessed on 24 October 2002.

[69]Oakley, 15.

[70]Walt, 1.

[71]McCormick, 68.

[72]Oakley, 16.

[73]Walt, 2.

[74]Douglas Brinkley, "Democratic Enlargement: The Clinton Doctrine," <u>Foreign Policy</u>, no. 106 (Spring 1997): 110-127 [database on-line]; available from Wilson Web; accessed 13 January 2003.

[75]Clinton, 1994 NSSR, 26.

[76]Warren Christopher, "Iraq Belongs on the Back Bruner," The New York Times, 31 December 2002; available from <http://www.nytimes.com/2002/12/31/opinion/31CHRI.html>; Internet; accessed 31 December 2002.

[77]Prunier, 101, 165.

[78]Walter Clarke and Jeffrey Herbst, Somalia and the Future of Humanitarian Intervention," Foreign Affairs 75, no. 2. (March /April 1996): 71.

[79]Melvern, 113.

[80]Barbara Crossette, "On Foreign Affairs, U.S. Public is Nontraditional," New York Times 28 Dec 1997. Available from <http://www.mtholyoke.edu/acad/intrel/pubop.htm>; Internet; accessed 24 November 2002.

[81]Ibid., 3.

[82]Walt, 11-12.

[83]Clarke, 71.

[84]Jack Nelson, and Doyle McManus, "Clinton: No Plant to Fire Christopher or Lake," Los Angeles Times 29 May 1994. Available from <http://www.tibet.ca/wtnarchive/1994/5/29_2.html>; Internet; accessed 11 December 2002.

[85]Ibid.

[86]Ibid.

[87]Michael Clough, "A President Bedeviled by a lack of Vision Foreign Affairs," Los Angeles Times 17 October 1993. p. 1 [database on-line]; available from ProQuest; accessed on 24 October 2002.

[88]Michael Dobbs, "Albright Approach: Upfront, Personal," Washington Post, 24 February 1997. Available from http://www.tibet.ca/wtnarchive/1994/5/29_2.html>; Internet; accessed 11 December 2002.

[89]Ibid.

[90]Ann Scott Tyson, "Three Musketeers of US Foreign Policy," The Christian Science Monitor, 20 February 1998. Available from <http://www.csmonitor.com/durable/1998/02/20/us/us.3.htmll>; Internet; accessed 11 December 2002.

[91]John E. Lange, "Civilian-Military Cooperation and Humanitarian Assistance: Lessons from Rwanda," Parameters Summer 1998 [journal online]; available from <http:/www.carlisle.army.mil/usawc/Parameteres/98summer/lange.htm>; Internet; accessed 10 September 2002.

[92]Department of Defense, "Discussion Paper Rwanda," Washington, D.C.: U.S. Department of Defense, 1 May 1994. Available from <http://www.gwu.edu/~nsarchiv/NSAEBB/NSAEBB53/rw050194.pdf>; Internet; accessed 24 November 2002 .

[93]Jacob Heibrunn, "The Great Equivocator," The New Republic, 216, no. 12 (24 March 1997): Available from <http://www.mtholyoke.edu/acad/intrel/lakedoc.html>; Internet; accessed 24 November 2002.

[94]Ibid.

[95]Ibid.

[96]Ibid.

[97]Congress, House of Representatives, Subcommittee on International Operations and Human Rights of the Committee on International Relations, Rwanda: Genocide and the Continuing Cycle of Violence, 105th Cong., 2d Sess., 5 May 1998, 16.

[98]Warren P. Stroble, "The CNN Effect," American Journalism Review. (May 1996). 32. [database on-line]; available from Nexis; accessed 26 October 2002.

[99]Lindey Hilsum, "Where is Kilgali?", Granta, (Autumn 1995):148.

[100]Joshua Hammer, "The Killing Fields," Newsweek 123, no. 21 (23 May 1994): 46. [database on-line]; available from EBSCO Host; accessed 20 December 2002.

[101]Congress, House of Representatives, 24.

[102]Nik Gowing, "Media Coverage: Help or Hindrance in Conflict Prevention," Carnegie Corporation of New York, NY. excerpt reprinted in U.S. Army War College, Course 2: "War, National Security Policy & Strategy Readings Vol I, (Carlisle Barracks, PA.. 30 July 2002), 304.

[103]Steven Livingston,. "Clarifying the CNN Effect: An Examination of Media Effects According to Type of Military Intervention," June 1997; available from < http://www.ksg.harvard.edu/presspol/publications/pdfs/70916_R-18.pdf>; Internet. accessed 11 December 2002.

[104]Stroble.

[105]Scott Webster, "President Bill Clinton's Foreign Policy: A Critical Assessment," Round Table Discussion. Co-Sponsored by the Center for the Advanced Study of Leadership and the Fulbright International Center, University of Maryland, 7 May 1999. Available from <www.academy.umd.edu/scholarship/casl/ Publications/Clinton_Roundtable.htm>; internet; accessed 17 January 2003.

[106]Webster.

[107]Nelson.

[108]Lake, Anthony, "From Containment to Enlargement," lecture, John Hoplins Universtiy , School of Advanced International Studies, 21 September 1993. Available from <http://www.mtholyoke.edu/acad/intrel/lakedoc.html>. Internet. Accessed 24 November 2002.

[109]Ibid.

[110]Clinton, 1994 NSSR, 2.

[111]Congressional Budget Office Report, 4.

[112]Oakley, 33 and Holly J Burkhalter, "The Question of Genocide: The Clinton Administration and Rwanda," The World Policy Journal, 11 (Winter 1994/1995): 44.

[113]Warren Christopher, "Iraq Belongs on the Back Burner," The New York Times 31 December 2002. Available from <http://www.nytimes.com/2002/12/31/opinion/31CHRI.html>; Internet; accessed 31 December 2002.

[114]William T. Johnsen, Deciphering the Balkan Enigma: Using History to Inform Policy (Strategic Studies Institute, Carlisle Barracks: U.S. Army War College, 1993), 4, 23.

[115]Agency for International Development, "Strategy for Kosovo 2001-2003," Available from <http://wwwusaid.gov/missions/kosovo/kosstat.htm>; Internet; accessed on 22 September 2002.

[116]Agency for International Development.

[117]Department of State, "Kosovo Chronology," 21 May 1999; available from <http:/www.state.gov/www/regions/ eur/fs_kosovo _timeline.html>; Internet; accessed 16 September 2002.

[118] NATO Homepage, "NATO's Role in Relation to the Conflict in Kosovo," 15 July 1999; Available from <http://www.nato.int.kosovo/history.htm>; Internet; accessed on 7 September 2002.

[119]Department of State, "Kosovo Chronology.

[120]NATO Homepage.

[121]Ibid.; Department of State.

[122]Department of State, "Fact Sheet: United Nations Interim Mission in Kosovo," 13 April 2001; available from <http:/www.state.gov/p/io/rls/fs/2001/2532pf.htm>; Internet; accessed 16 September 2002.

[123]Stewart Patrick, "Don't Fence Me In," World Policy Journal. Fall 2001. [journal on-line]; available from <http://www.worldpolicy.org/journal/sum01-3.html>; Internet; accessed on 12 December 2002.

[124]Ibid.

[125]Ibid.

[126]William J. Clinton, <u>A National Security Strategy for a Global Age</u> (Washington D.C.: The White House, December 2000), 5.

[127]William J. Clinton, "Statement to the Nation," in <u>The Clinton Foreign Policy Reader,</u> Rubinstein, Alvin Z., Shayevich, Albiana and Zlotnikov, Boris, eds. Armonk (NY. M.E. Sharpe, 2000), 190.

[128]Jimmy Carter, "Have We Forgotten the Path to Peace?," <u>The New York Times</u> 27 May 1999, sec A, p. 33 (1071 words) [database on-line]; available from Nexis; assessed 29 January 2003.

[129]William J. Clinton, <u>A National Security Strategy for a New Century</u> (Washington D.C.: The White House, October 1998), 37.

[130]Ivo H. Daalder, "And Now, A Clinton Doctrine?," <u>Foreign Policy Studies in Print</u> 10 July 1999, Available from < http://www.brook.edu/dybdocroot/views/op-ed/daalder/19990710.htm>; Internet; accessed 23 November 2002.

[131]Wesley K. Clark, <u>Waging Modern War: Bosnia, Kosovo ad the Future of Combat</u> (New York: Public Affairs, 2001), xxiv.

[132]Ibid.

[133]Walter Isaacson, "Madeline's War," <u>Time</u> 153 (17 May 1999): 26 [Database on-line]; available from Wilson Web; accessed on 15 December 2002.

[134]Ibid.

[135]Michael Hirsh, "At War with Ourselves," <u>Harper's</u> 299 (July 1999):60 [database on-line]; available from Wilson Web; accessed on 15 December 2002.

[136]Ibid.; Barton Gellman, "The Path to Crisis: How the United States and Its Allies Went to War," <u>The Washington Post</u> 18 April 1999, (4646 words) [database on-line]; available from Lexis-Nexis; assessed 19 January 2003.

[137]Hirsh.

[138]Ibid.

[139]Ibid.

[140]Gellman.

[141]Ibid.

[142]Isaacson.

[143]David Halberstam, <u>War in a Time of peace</u> (New York, NY:Scribner, 2001), 273

[144]David Reiff, "A New Hierarch of Values and Interests," <u>World Policy Journal</u> 16, no. 3 (Fall 1999): 28-34. [database on-line]; available from Wilson Web; accessed on 27 November 2002.

[145]James Bennet, "Analysis: Clinton's Foreign Policy Crystallized," <u>New York Times</u> 1 May 1998; available from < http://www.mtholyoke.edu/acad/intrel/expwins.htm>; internet; accessed 24 November 2002.

[146]Blaine Harden, and John Broder, "Clinton Tries to Win the War and Keep the U.S. Voters Content," <u>New York Times</u> 22 May 1999; available from <http://www.mtholyoke.edu/acad/intrel/harden.htm>; Internet; accessed 13 December 2002.

[147]K.P. Foley, "NATO: Many Remain Skeptical of Clinton Balkan Policy," <u>Radio Free Europe</u> 25 March 1999; available from <http://www.rferl.org/nca/features/1999/03/F.RU.990325143952>. Internet; accessed on 13 December 2002.

[148]Terrance Hunt, "Kosovo Hurts Clinton in Polls," <u>Southcoast Today</u> 29 May 1999; Available from <http:/www.s-t.com/daily/05-99/05-29-99/a09wn055.htm>; Internet; accessed 13 December 2002.

[149]Ibid.

[150]American Enterprise Institute, "Public Opinion on Kosovo," Available from <http://www.aei.org/Kosovo.htm>; Internet; accessed 13 January 2003.

[151]Hunt.

[152]R. W. Apple Jr., "Deep Concern in the World Over Weakened Clinton," <u>New York Times</u> 25 September 1998; Available from < http://www.mtholyoke.edu/acad/intrel/hegcon.htm>; Internet; accessed 24 November 2002.

[153]Jesse Jackson, "Two Continents," <u>The Wilson Quarterly</u> 23 no. 314 (Summer 1999): 22 [database on-line]; available from Wilson Web; accessed 15 December 2002.

[154]Sherry Ricchiardi, "Searching for Truth in the Balkans," <u>American Journalism Review</u> (June 1999): 22-28. [database on-line]; available from ProQuest; accessed 15 December 2002.

[155]Jamie P. Shea, "The Kosovo Crisis and the Media," <u>NATO's Nations and Partners for Peace 2000</u> 1 [database on-line]; available from ProQuest; accessed on 15 December 2002.

[156]Ibid.

[157]Gellman.

[158]Linda D Kozaryn, "Albright Says Kosovo Matters to United States," <u>America Forces Information Service</u> 8 February 1999; Available from

<http://www.defenselink.mil/news/Feb1999/n02081999_9902084.html>; Internet; accessed 7 January 2003.

[159]Ibid.

[160]Ibid.

[161]Roskin, 65.

[162]Harden.

[163]Ibid.

[164]Christopher Layne, "Blunder in the Balkans," The CATO Institute; Available from <http://www.cato.org/pubs/pas/pa-345es.html>; Internet; accessed on 13 December 2002.

[165]Rubinstein, 7.

[166]The USS Harlan County was a cargo ship turned back from docking at Port-au-Prince, Haiti in 1994 by a group supporting General Raul Cedras. The event was another situation in which U.S. foreign policy looked impotent and was a major foreign policy embarrassment for the Clinton administration.

[167]Halberstam, 276.

[168]Clinton, 2000 NSSR, 5.

[169]Hirsh, 6.

[170]Halberstam, 386.

[171]Isaacson.

[172]Tyson.

[173]Gowing, 304.

[174]McCormick, 72.

[175]Rubinstein, 171.

[176]Halberstam, 273.

[177]Clinton, 1994 NSSR, 26.

BIBLIOGRAPHY

Ajami, Fouad. "Home Base," The New Republic. 224, no. 23, (4 June 2001): Database on-line. Available from Wilson Web. Accessed 27 November 2002.

American Enterprise Institute. "Public Opinion on Kosovo." Available from <http://www.aei.org/Kosovo.htm>. Internet. Accessed 13 January 2003.

Apple, R.W. Jr.. "Deep Concern in the World Over Weakened Clinton." New York Times, 25 September 1998. Available from < http://www.mtholyoke.edu/acad/intrel/hegcon.htm>. Internet. Accessed 24 November 2002

Bennet, James. "Analysis: Clinton's Foreign Policy Crystallized." New York Times, 1 May 1998. Available from < http://www.mtholyoke.edu/acad/intrel/expwins.htm>. Internet. Accessed 24 November 2002.

_____. "President Urges More U.S. Involvement in World Affairs." New York Times, 12 April 1997. Available from < http://www.mtholyoke.edu/acad/intrel/clinenga.htm>. Internet. Accessed 24 November 2002.

Brinkley,Douglas. "Democratic Enlargement: The Clinton Doctrine." Foreign Policy, no. 106 (Spring 1997): 110-127. Database on-line. Available from Wilson Web. Accessed 13 January 2003.

Burkhalter, Holly J. "The Question of Genocide: The Clinton Administration and Rwanda." The World Policy Journal 11 (Winter 1994/1995): 44-54.

Burns, James. "President Bill Clinton's Foreign Policy: A Critical Assessment." Round Table Discussion. Co-Sponsored by the Center for the Advanced Study of Leadership and the Fulbright International Center, University of Maryland, 7 May 1999. Available from <www.academy.umd.edu/scholarship/casl/ Publications/Clinton_Roundtable.htm>. Internet. Accessed 17 January 2003.

Bush, George W. The National Security Strategy of the United States of America Washington, D.C.: The White House, September 2002.

Carr, Damian P. "U.S. Army Public Affairs During Operation Uphold Democracy." Masters Thesis, U.S. Army Command and General Staff College, 1996.

Carter, Jimmy. "Have We Forgotten the Path to Peace?." The New York Times, 27 May 1999, sec A, p. 33 (1071 words). Database on-line. Available from Nexis. Assessed 29 January 2003.

Cerami, Joeseph R., and Holcomb, James F. Jr., eds. U.S. Army War College Guide to Strategy. Carlisle Barracks, PA: Strategic Studies Institute, U.S. Army War College, 2001.

Christopher, Warren. "Iraq Belongs on the Back Burner." The New York Times, 31 December 2002. Available from <http://www.nytimes.com/2002/12/31/opinion/31CHRI.html>. Internet. Accessed 31 December 2002.

Clark, Wesley K. Waging Modern War: Bosnia, Kosovo and the Future of Combat. New York, NY: Public Affairs, 2001.

Clarke, Walter and Herbst, Jeffrey. Somalia and the Future of Humanitarian Intervention." Foreign Affairs 75, no. 2. (March /April 1996): 70-85.

Clinton, William J. A National Security Strategy for a Global Age. Washington D.C.: The White House, December 2000.

_____. A National Security Strategy for a New Century. Washington, D.C.: The White House, December 1999.

_____. A National Security Strategy for a New Century. Washington D.C.: The White House, October 1998.

_____. A National Security Strategy for a New Century. Washington, D.C.: The White House, May 1997.

_____. A National Security Strategy of Engagement and Enlargement. Washington, D.C.: The White House, February 1996.

_____. A National Security Strategy of Engagement and Enlargement. Washington, D.C.: The White House, February 1995.

_____. A National Security Strategy of Engagement and Enlargement. Washington D.C.: The White House, July 1994.

_____. Presidential Decision Directive 25, Reforming Multilateral Peace Operations. Washington, D.C.: The White House, 6 May 1994. Available from <http:/www.fas.org/irp/offdocs/pdd25.html>. Internet. Accessed 22 September 2002.

Clough, Michael. "A President Bedeviled by a lack of Vision." Los Angeles Times, 17 October 1993, [database on-line]; available from ProQuest; accessed 24 October 2002.

Collier, Ellen C. Instances of Unites States Forces Abroad. 1798-1993. Washington, D.C.: Congressional Research Service, October 1993. Available from < http://www.history.navy.mil/wars/foabroad.htm>. Internet. Accessed 24 November 2002.

Crossette. Barbara. "On Foreign Affairs, U.S. Public is Nontraditional," The New York Times, 28 December 1997. Available from <http://www.mtholyoke.edu/acad/intrel/pubop.htm>. Internet. Accessed 24 November 2002.

Daalder, Ivo H. "And Now, a Clinton Doctrine?." Foreign Policy Studies in Print, 10 July 1999. Available from < http://www.brook.edu/dybdocroot/views/op-ed/daalder/19990710.htm>. Internet. Accessed 23 November 2002.

Deibel, Terry, L. "Clinton and Congress: The Politics of Foreign Policy." Foreign Policy Association Headline Series, 321 (Fall 2000)

Dobbs, Michael. Albright Approach: Upfront , Personal," The Washington Post, 24 February 1997. Available from <http://www.tibet.ca/wtnarchive/1994/5/29_2.html>. Internet. Accessed 11 December 2002.

Dorf, Robert H. "Some Basic Concepts and Approaches to the Study of International Politics." In U.S. Army War College Guide to Strategy, ed. Joseph R. Cerami and James F. Holcomb Jr., 31-41. Carlisle Barracks, PA: Strategic Studies Institute, U.S. Army War College, 2001.

Feil, Scott R. Preventing Genocide: How the Early Use of Force Might Have Succeeded in Rwanda. A Report to the Carnegie Commission on Preventing Deadly Conflict, New York: Carnegie Corporation, 1998.

Foley, K. P. "NATO: Many Remain Skeptical of Clinton Balkan Policy," Radio Free Europe. 25 March 1999. Available from <http://www.rferl.org/nca/features/1999/03/F.RU.990325143952>. Internet. Accessed 13 December 2002.

Gellman, Barton. "The Path to Crisis: How the United States and Its Allies Went to War," The Washington Post, 18 April 1999, sec A, p. 1 (4646 words). Database on-line. Available from Lexis-Nexis. Assessed 19 January 2003.

Gowing, Nik. "Media Coverage: Help or Hindrance in Conflict Prevention." Carnegie Corporation of New York, NY. Excerpt reprinted in U.S. Army War College, Course 2: "War, National Security Policy & Strategy Readings Vol. I Carlisle Barracks, PA.: 30 July 2002.

Grant-Wisdom, Dorith. "President Bill Clinton's Foreign Policy: A Critical Assessment." Round Table Discussion. Co-Sponsored by the Center for the Advanced Study of Leadership and the Fulbright International Center, University of Maryland, 7 May 1999. Available from <www.academy.umd.edu/scholarship/casl/ Publications/Clinton_Roundtable.htm>. Internet. Accessed 17 January 2003.

Halberstam, David. War in a Time of peace. New York, NY: Scribner, 2001.

Hammer, Joshua. "The Killing Fields." Newsweek, 23 May 1994, 46. Database on-line. Available from EBSCO Host. Accessed 20 December 2002.

Harden, Blaine and Broder, John. "Clinton Tries to Win the War and Keep the U.S. Voters Content." New York Times, 22 May 1999. Available from http://www.mtholyoke.edu/acad/intrel/harden.htm>. Internet. Accessed 13 December 2002

Heibrunn, Jacob. "The Great Equivocator." The New Republic, 216, no.12 (24 March 1997): Available from <http://www.mtholyoke.edu/acad/intrel/lakedoc.html>. Internet. Accessed 24 November 2002.

Hilsum, Lindey. "Where is Kilgali?." Granta, Autumn 1995.

Hirsh, Michael. "At War with Ourselves." Harper's, 299, no. 1790, (July 1999): 60-69. Database on-line. Available from Wilson Web. Accessed 15 December 2002.

Holmes, Kim R. "Humanitarian Warriors: The Moral Follies of the Clinton Doctrine" 11 July 2000; Available from <http://www.heritage.org/Research/NationalSecurity/hl671.cfm>. Accessed 22 September 2002.

Human Rights Watch. "Human Rights Watch World Report 2001: Rwanda: The Role of the International Community." Available from <http://www.hrw.org/wr2kl/Africa/rwanda3.html>. Internet. Accessed 8 October 2002.

Hunt, Terrance. "Kosovo Hurts Clinton in Polls." Southcoast Today, 29 May 1999. Available from <http:/www.s-t.com/daily/05-99/05-29-99/a09wn055.htm>. Internet. Accessed13 December 2002.

Ilsaacson, Walter. "Madeline's War," Time 153, no.19 (17 May 1999): 26-35. Database on-line. Available from Wilson Web. Internet. Accessed15 December 2002.

Jablonsky, David. "The Persistence of Credibility: Interests, Threats and Planning for the Use of American Military Power." In U.S. Army War College Guide to Strategy, ed. Joseph R. Cerami and James F. Holcomb Jr., 43-54. Carlisle Barracks, PA: Strategic Studies Institute, U.S. Army War College, 2001.

Jackson, Jesse. "Two Continents." The Wilson Quarterly 23 no. 314 (Summer 1999): 14. Database on-line. Available from Wilson Web. Accessed 15 December 2002.

Joffe, Josef. "Clinton's World: Purpose, Policy and Weltanschauung." Washington Quarterly 24 no. 1 (Winter 2001): Database on-line. Available from EBSCO Host. Accessed 27 November 2002.

Johnsen, William T. Deciphering the Balkan Enigma: Using History to Inform Policy. Strategic Studies Institute, Carlisle Barracks: U.S. Army War College, 1993.

Kellerman, Barbara. "President Bill Clinton's Foreign Policy: A Critical Assessment." Round Table Discussion. Co-Sponsored by the Center for the Advanced Study of Leadership and the Fulbright International Center, University of Maryland, 7 May 1999. Available from <www.academy.umd.edu/scholarship/casl/ Publications/Clinton_Roundtable.htm>. Internet. Accessed 17 January 2003.

KFOR On-line. "KFOR Objectives/Missions." 22 September 2002. Available from <http://www.nato.int/kfor/for/objectives.htm>. Internet. Accessed 22 September 2002.

Kolodziej, Edward A. The Great Powers and Genocide: Lessons form Rwanda Arms Control, Disarmament, and International Security Occasional Paper Series. Champaign, University of Illinois, 2000

Kozaryn, Linda D. "Albright Says Kosovo Matters to United States." America Forces Information Service 8 February 1999. Available from <http://www.defenselink.mil/news/Feb1999/n02081999_9902084.html>. Internet. Accessed 7 January 2003.

Kuperman, Alan J. The Limits of Humanitarian Intervention. Washington, D.C.: Brookings Institution Press, 2001.

Lake, Anthony, "From Containment to Enlargement," Lecture, John Hopkins University, School of Advanced International Studies, 21 September 1993. Available from <http://www.mtholyoke.edu/acad/intrel/lakedoc.html>. Internet. Accessed 24 November 2002.

Lampe, John R. "President Bill Clinton's Foreign Policy: A Critical Assessment." Round Table Discussion. Co-Sponsored by the Center for the Advanced Study of Leadership and the Fulbright International Center, University of Maryland, 7 May 1999. Available from <www.academy.umd.edu/scholarship/casl/ Publications/Clinton_Roundtable.htm>. Internet. Accessed 17 January 2003.

Lange, John E. "Civilian-Military Cooperation and Humanitarian Assistance: Lesson from Rwanda." Parameters (Summer 1998): 106-122. Available from <http:/www.carlisle.army.mil/usawc/Parameters/98summer/lange.htm> Internet. Accessed 26 October 2002.

Layne, Christopher. "Blunder in the Balkans," Policy Analysis, The CATO Institute. Available from <http://www.cato.org/pubs/pas/pa-345es.html>. Internet. Accessed 13 December 2002.

Lilley, James R. "President Bill Clinton's Foreign Policy: A Critical Assessment." Round Table Discussion. Co-Sponsored by the Center for the Advanced Study of Leadership and the Fulbright International Center, University of Maryland, 7 May 1999. Available from <www.academy.umd.edu/scholarship/casl/ Publications/Clinton_Roundtable.htm>. Internet. Accessed 17 January 2003.

Livingston, Steven. "Clarifying the CNN Effect: An Examination of Media Effects According to Type of Military Intervention" June 1997. Available from < http://www.ksg.harvard.edu/presspol/publications/pdfs/70916_R-18.pdf>. Internet. Accessed 11 December 2002.

Maynes, Charles William. "Bottom-Up Foreign Policy," Foreign Policy no. 104 (Fall 1996). Available from <http://www.mtholyoke.edu/acad/intrel/maynes.htm>. Internet. Accessed 24 November 2002.

McCormick, James M. "Clinton and Foreign Policy." In The Postmodern Presidency, ed. Steven E. Schier, ed. 6-83. Pittsburgh, PA: University of Pittsburgh Press, 2000.

Melvern, Linda. A People Betrayed: The Role of the West in Rwanda's Genocide. New York: Zed Books LTD, 2000.

Metz, Steven. Disaster and Intervention in Sub-Saharan Africa: Learning from Rwanda Strategic Studies Institute, Carlisle Barracks: U.S. Army War College, 1994. Available from <http://www.carlisle.army.mil/ssi/pubs/1994/rwanda/rwanda.htm>. Internet. Accessed 24 November 2002.

NATO Homepage. "NATO's Role in Relation to the Conflict in Kosvo." 15 July 1999. Available from <http://www.nato.int.kosovo/history.htm>. Internet. Accessed 7 September 2002.

Nelson, Jack and McManus, Doyle. "Clinton: No Plan to Fire Christopher or Lake," <u>Los Angeles Times,</u> 29 May 1994. Available from <http://www.tibet.ca/ntarchive/1994/5/29_2.html>. Internet. Accessed 11 December 2002.

Neuchterlein, Donald E. "Defining U.S. National Interests: An Analytical Framework." In <u>America Overcommitted: Unites States National Interests in the 1980s.</u> University of Kentucky Press, Lexington, KY. Excerpt reprinted in U.S. Army War College, Course 2: "War, National Security Policy & Strategy Readings Vol I, Carlisle Barracks, PA: 30 July 2002.

Oakley, Robert B. and Tucker, David. <u>Two Perspectives on Interventions and Humanitarian Operations.</u> Strategic Studies Institute, U.S. Army War College, 1997.

Organization for African Unity. <u>Report on Rwandan Genocide, Executive Summary</u> June 2000. Provided by COL Thomas A. Dempsey, Faculty Instructor, U.S. Army War College, Carlisle Barracks, PA. 2002.

Patrick, Stewart. "Don't Fence Me In." <u>World Policy Journal</u> Fall 2001. Journal on-line. onAvailable from <http://www.worldpolicy.org/journal/sum01-3.html>. Internet. Accessed 12 December 2002.

Prunier. Gerard. <u>The Rwanda Crisis: History of a Genocide.</u> New York: Columbia University Press, 1995.

Reiff, David, "A New Hierarch of Values and Interests," <u>World Policy Journal</u> 16, no. 3 (Fall 1999): 28-34. Database On-line. Available from Wilson Web. Accessed 27 November 2002.

Ricchiardi, Sherry. "Searching for Truth in the Balkans," <u>American Journalism Review</u> 21, no.5 (June 1999): 22-28. Database on-line. Available from ProQuest. Accessed 15 December 2002.

Rosen, Gary. "Can We Prevent Genocide?," <u>Commentary</u> 107, no. 2, (February 1999): 51. Database on-line. Available from EBSCO Host. Accessed 18 November 2002.

Roskin, Michael G. Roskin. "National Interest: From Abstraction to Strategy." In <u>U.S. Army War College Guide to Strategy</u>, ed. Joseph R. Cerami and James F. Holcomb Jr., 55-67. Carlisle Barracks, PA: Strategic Studies Institute, U.S. Army War College, 2001.

Rubinstein, Alvin Z., Shayevich, Albiana and Zlotnikov, Boris, eds. <u>The Clinton Foreign Policy Reader.</u> Armonk, NY. M.E. Sharpe, 2000.

Sciolinio, Elaine. "Berger is Manager of Crises, Not Global Strategy," <u>New York Times</u>, 18 May 1998. Available from < http://www.mtholyoke.edu/acad/intrel/berger.htm>. Internet. Accessed 24 November 2002.

Shea, Jamie P. "The Kosovo Crisis and the Media." <u>NATO's Nations and Partners for Peace</u>, 2000. Database on-line. Available from ProQuest. Accessed 15 December 2002.

Sisk, Timothy D. "Violence: Intrastate Conflict." <u>Managing Global issues: Lessons Learned</u> Washington DC: Carnegie Endowment for International Peace. Simmons P.J. and Oudraat, Chantal de Jonge, eds. Washington, D.C. Excerpt reprinted in U.S. Army War

College, Course 2: "War, National Security Policy & Strategy Readings Vol IV, Carlisle Barracks, PA: 30 July 2002.

Snider, Don M. and Nagel, John A. "The National Security Strategy: Documenting a Vision." In <u>U.S. Army War College Guide to Strategy</u>, ed. Joseph R. Cerami and James F. Holcomb Jr., 127-142. Carlisle Barracks, PA: Strategic Studies Institute, U.S. Army War College, 2001.

Steel, Ronald. "The Domestic Core of Foreign Policy." <u>The Atlantic Monthly</u>. Volume 275, no. 6 (June 1995): 84-92.

Stroble, Waren P. "The CNN Effect." <u>American Journalism Review</u> (May 1996): 32 (3678 words). Database on-line. Available from Nexis. Accessed 26 October 2002.

Trueheart, Charles, "France Faults U.S., U.N. in Rwanda Genocide." <u>The Washington Post</u>, 16 December 1998, Sec. A, p. 37. Database on-line. Available from ProQuest. Accessed 27 September 2002.

Tyson, Ann Scott, "Three Musketeers of US Foreign Policy." <u>The Christian Science Monitor</u>, 20 February 1998. Available from <http://www.csmonitor.com/durable/1998/02/20/us/us.3.htmll>. Internet. Accessed 11 December 2002.

U.S. Agency for International Development. "Strategy for Kosovo 2001-2003." Available from <http://wwwusaid.gov/missions/kosovo/kosstat.htm>. Internet. Accessed on 22 September 2002.

U.S. Congress. House of Representatives. Subcommittee on International Operations and Human Rights of the Committee on International Relations. <u>Rwanda: Genocide and the Continuing Cycle of Violence</u>. 105th Cong., 2d Sess., 5 May 1998.

U.S. Congressional Budget Office Report. Making Peace While Staying Ready for War: The Challenges of U.S. Military Participation in Peace Operations. Washington, D.C.: Congressional Budget Office, December 1999. Available from <http:/www.cbo.gov/showdoc.cfm?index+1809&sequence =2>. Internet. Accessed 22 September 2002.

U.S. Department of Defense. "Discussion Paper Rwanda" Washington, D.C.: U.S. Department of Defense, 1May 1994. . Available from <http://www.gwu.edu/~nsarchiv/NSAEBB/NSAEBB53/rw050194.pdf>. Internet. Accessed 24 November 2002.

U.S. Department of State. "Kosovo Chronology," 21 May 1999. Available from <http:/www.state.gov/www/regions/ eur/fs_kosovo _timeline.html>. Internet. Accessed 16 September 2002.

U.S. Department of State. "Fact Sheet: United Nations Interim Mission in Kosovo," 13 April 2001. Available from <http:/www.state.gov/p/io/rls/fs/2001/2532pf.htm>. Internet. Accessed 16 September 2002.

Walt, Stephen M. "Two Cheers for Clinton's Foreign Policy," <u>Foreign Affairs</u>, 79, no. 2 (March/April 2000). Journal on-line. Available from <ttp://www.foreignpolicy2000.org/library/issuebriefs/readingnotes/fa_walt.html>. Internet. Accessed 24 October 2002.

Webster, Scott. "President Bill Clinton's Foreign Policy: A Critical Assessment." Round Table Discussion. Co-Sponsored by the Center for the Advanced Study of Leadership and the Fulbright International Center, University of Maryland, 7 May 1999. Available from <www.academy.umd.edu/scholarship/casl/ Publications/Clinton_Roundtable.htm>. Internet. Accessed 17 January 2003.

www.ingramcontent.com/pod-product-compliance
Lightning Source LLC
Chambersburg PA
CBHW080610290526
45790CB00007B/2721